NOTES OF A NON-CONSPIRATOR

NOTES OF A NON-CONSPIRATOR

Working with Russian Dissidents

ALLAN WYNN

ANDRE DEUTSCH

Notes of a Non-Conspirator is also the title of the autobiography of Efim Etkind, translated by Peter France, published by Oxford University Press, 1978 (now out of print).

The late Dr Allan Wynn was unaware of the previous use of this phrase which, like Mr Etkind or his translator, he devised spontaneously for his own book. In view of the perfect aptness of the title, André Deutsch concurs with the Wynn family's decision to publish this book under the title its author originally intended.

First published in 1987 by
André Deutsch Limited
105–106 Great Russell Street London WC1B 3LJ

British Library Cataloguing in Publication Data

Wynn, Allan
Notes of a non-conspirator : working with
Russian dissidents.
1. Dissenters—Soviet Union—History—
20th century 2. International agencies
I. Title
364.1'31   HV8959.S65

ISBN 0 233 98149 7

Printed in Great Britain by
The St Edmundsbury Press
Bury St Edmunds, Suffolk

CONTENTS

ACKNOWLEDGEMENTS

The author and publisher would like to thank the following for permission to quote: – The Bodley Head (*Yawning Heights* by Alexander Zinoviev, trans. by Gordon Clough, 1979); Collins Harvill (*Hope Against Hope*, 1961, and *Hope Abandoned*, 1974, by Nadezhda Mandelstam, trans. by Max Hayward; *This Is Moscow Speaking and Other Stories* by Yuli Daniel, trans. by Max Hayward, 1968; *The Makepeace Experiment* by Abram Tertz, trans. by Manya Harari, 1977; *The Trial Begins* by Abram Tertz, trans. by Max Hayward, 1960); Faber & Faber (*Vaclav Havel or Living in Truth*, ed. Jan Vadislav, 1986); Grafton Books (*Poems* by Osip Mandelstam, chosen and translated by James Greene, Paul Elek, 1980); *Guardian*; *New York Times*; W. W. Norton & Co., Inc. (*Poems* by Anna Akhmatova, selected and translated by Lyn Coffin, 1983); Oxford University Press (*Selected Poems* by Osip Mandelstam, trans. by Clarence Brown & W. S. Merwin, OUP 1973/Penguin 1977); *Washington Post* (article by Kevin Klose).

INTRODUCTION

'There are no internal affairs left on this cramped globe of ours. Mankind can only be saved if everybody takes an interest in everybody else's affairs; if the people of the East cease to be indifferent to what is thought in the West, and if people in the West cease to be indifferent to what is happening in the East.'

Alexander Solzhenitsyn, from his speech on the occasion of the award to him of the Nobel Prize.

Over a period of fourteen years, starting in 1973, I became drawn into the campaign to bring human rights to the people of the USSR. These notes are a record of that activity. They are derived from diary entries, articles, memos and letters written at the time. Since my diary entries were mainly *aides-memoire*, brief and non-descriptive, it has been necessary to provide footnotes and other explanatory material but I have not altered comments and opinions in the light of hindsight, even when, as has not infrequently been the case, time has proved them wrong. I wish to acknowledge that most of the activity which is described was the work of other people, many of whom have had scant if any acknowledgement of their contribution to a struggle which clearly lies at the heart of mankind's hopes for peace and for survival.

PART ONE
Explaining Soviet Reality

CHAPTER 1

THE RELUCTANT ACTIVIST:
The Panov Affair

'What the hell am I doing here?' I asked myself. I was shivering with cold and feeling slightly ridiculous holding a flaming torch in one hand and a placard saying 'Let the Panovs Go' in the other.

I suppose there were about twenty of us in a bedraggled group at the entrance to the driveway off the Bayswater Road which leads to the Soviet embassy. It was a cold January night in 1973. A policeman controlled the entry into the embassy driveway; he was tall, warmly-clad, good-tempered and unbothered. He gave a sense of reality to what otherwise seemed to be a charade gone somewhat haywire. Members of the embassy staff came and went, seemingly indifferent to our presence. Of course, protests of one sort or another were an almost daily event outside the Soviet embassy. No doubt, there was a lot to protest about.

'Would you hang on to these for a jiffy?' I said to a duffle-coated young woman in our group who was at that moment empty handed, and leaving her with my torch and placard, I took off up the Bayswater Road past the concrete monstrosity of the Czech embassy (certainly the ugliest building in London if not in the entire universe). Gratefully, I sank into a cubicle in the salt beef bar. A hot, rich, fat-laden corned beef sandwich and a cup of coffee revived my spirits. I reviewed the situation.

It had all started in the most unlikely of places, the crush bar at Covent Garden. During the interval of a ballet performance an acquaintance, Rosemary Winckley, joined my wife and myself for what I thought was to be a quiet drink; but as it turned out Rosemary took the opportunity to make a spirited demand that we should join the committee she had formed to help free the Panovs. Rosemary had a fierce dedication to freedom, and an emotional attachment (one might even speak of passion, but let attachment suffice) to the person of Valery Panov, then the leading character dancer of the Kirov Ballet Company. My wife,

Sally Gilmour, had once been the principal dancer of the Ballet Rambert. But, sympathetic as she was to Rosemary's cause, she declined to join the committee because of a dislike for committees in general and protests in particular. She said I should join. After all, that's what husbands were mainly for – to protect their wives from unpleasant but necessary commitments. She promised (and amply delivered) moral support. My contribution was to be practical.

'Why not leave it to Woody Allen?' I ventured. 'Poking fun at the Russians and their idiotic attempts to suppress intellectual freedom should do the trick in the end.' This comment evoked no response. We resumed our seats. I had become, willy-nilly, a member of the Panov Committee. Actually, at that time I sub-scribed to the widely held view that a concern for Soviet dissidents was largely a CIA ploy fostered by the American arms industry. Simply a means of hotting up the cold war and generating profitable business. I don't doubt that to some degree this is in fact the case. But it is a long way from the whole story. In time I came to perceive Soviet communism, through experience of it, as representing a threat to civilization itself.

The brutal way in which Valery Panov and his wife, Galina, were being treated was, of course, widely known and greatly deplored. Obviously the Kirov Ballet Company had reason to fear further defections for, despite the fact that it was the custodian of the great ballet traditions of the Mariynsky Theatre, stifling bureaucratic mismanagement had caused first its finest choreogra-pher, Balanchine and, later, its great stars – Nureyev, Baryshnikov and Makarova – to defect to the West. Now Valery Panov had discovered a Jewish grandmother and was demanding the right to emigrate to Israel with his wife. Family re-unification is more or less recognized as conferring a right to emigrate in the USSR but the authorities claimed that Galina, who was 100% Russian, could not emigrate without her mother's permission, and this (due to a little persuasion from the KGB) was not forthcoming. But the Panovs were not easily deterred; they persisted in their demands and were dismissed after a humiliating dressing down in front of the whole company. They then found themselves in a classic 'catch 22' situation: forbidden to work, they were hounded for 'parisi-tism' – i.e. not working.

But the KGB had not taken Rosemary Winckley into their

calculations. Rosemary had got to know the Panovs pretty well on weekend trips to Leningrad. Besides being a balletomane, she was also the sister-in-law of Clive Barnes, at that time the most influential theatre critic in the US. But these were peripheral assets. The real source of her power was her unlimited energy and commitment. First she formed a committee of six women (I was allowed to be treasurer in the mistaken belief that women do not understand money but that I did. Otherwise I had no special role). Lady Diana Cooper was the patron and her great name helped enormously in gaining Rosemary access to practically every theatrical notable, visiting or resident, in London.

A few days before our midnight vigil, Rosemary had mobilized several hundred theatricals to march in procession from Speakers' Corner to the Soviet embassy. The procession was led by Anton Dolin, the first great English male ballet dancer, and included Laurence Olivier, Ralph Richardson, Paul Scofield and Claire Bloom. On arrival at the embassy an attempt was made to hand in a petition demanding exit permits for the Panovs. But the embassy official refused to accept it.

'Give it to me,' said Olivier, who marched up to the door and knocked on it loudly.

'Who's there?' came a voice from behind the firmly closed door.

'Lord Olivier.'

The door was opened at once, Olivier was ushered in and the petition delivered.

'The Russians adore aristocrats,' Olivier explained later with his disarming smile. 'They are the only people left who do.'

Bolstered by salt beef and coffee, I thought it time to get back to the demonstration but by then most of my fellow demonstrators had gone home and I decided to do likewise.

The Panov campaign was carried on through 1974 with petitions, letter writing, protest rallies, vigils and so on. But the most effective step was a threat by Actors Equity to ban the Bolshoi and other Soviet theatrical groups on which the Soviet government set great store for their propaganda value. The Panovs were allowed to emigrate in June 1975. Valery is at present Director of the Belgium National Ballet Company; Galina performs with this company but is also in great demand as a soloist all over the world.

The release of the Panovs was an important indication that Soviet power, despite its brutal image and its reputation for inflexibility, could be forced into humanitarian gestures by strong and persistent external pressure. What the world clearly needs to make it safe from tyranny is people like Rosemary Winckley. The question is – are there enough of them?

CHAPTER 2

THE POET WITNESSES

Shortly after I became a half-hearted member of the Panov Committee, my view of Soviet reality and the danger it posed to what I considered to be civilized values changed drastically. During my service as a naval officer (doctor) with the occupation forces in Japan (1945–7), I had come in contact with some reactionary American officers who were talking freely of the next war against the Soviet Union. Many of them thought it not only inevitable but also desirable. They made my blood run cold.

I had always regarded anti-communist crusaders with considerable suspicion. I was prepared to accept the excesses of Stalinism as a temporary aberration, feeling that the fact that the Revolution had occurred while the country was still dominated by a backward peasant-based agriculture and a poorly developed industrial system had made it inevitable that harsh measures would be required. Clearly Stalin had not hesitated to apply them and, equally clearly, his methods had involved a complete disregard for legality and dispensed cruelty and arbitrariness on an unheard of scale. But I did not believe that this was something inherent in communism itself.

Plenty of people still accept this argument. But I was to discover that most of these apologists have acquired their convictions from the teachings of social science departments of universities and colleges in the West. There were not many committed believers among the actual population of the Soviet Union or, for that matter, any other Marxist state.

My education into the nature of Soviet reality began by accident. I had gone to a reading at the Poetry Society in Earl's Court and, being early, I went for a drink at the bar. But I found no one there whom I knew and, since the habitués do not talk to strangers, I wandered into the library to browse. A book of Anna Akhmatova's poems was lying on a table and I picked it up, attracted by the introduction by Andrei Sinyavsky, some of whose books I had read, and whose fate (he was imprisoned and forced into exile for writing them) I had deplored.

Akhmatova's poetry, which moved me by its simplicity, simple imagery and passion, in some ways resembled Japanese *haiku*. For example:

> I am happy. But what I hold most dear,
> Is the sloping forest path,
> The simple crooked bridge,
> And that the days left to wait are few.

After a quarrel with a lover she wrote:

> Then be accursed. I will not touch
> Your damned soul with a groan or a glance.
> But I swear to you by the gardens of the angels,
> I swear by the miracle working icon,
> And by the fire and smoke of our nights,
> That I will never return.

I thought this great stuff although I suspected that, had it been submitted to the Poetry Society for publication, it would have been consigned to the wastepaper basket.

Next day I arranged to borrow the book and another, the poems of Osip Mandelstam, who was, as the librarian explained, a close friend of Akhmatova's. I found both poets equally stimulating and this led me to the memoir of Mandelstam, *Hope against Hope*, written by his wife, Nadezhda (Nadia). This poignant book left me wondering to what extent the horrendous reality it portrayed reflected the present Soviet state. Was the callous treatment of the Panovs an isolated phenomenon, due essentially to bureaucratic insensitivity, or did it reflect something more profoundly anti-humanist? I determined to try and find out.

I knew, of course, how difficult it is for an outsider to gain real insight into a society of which he is not a part. Russia, with its unique history, its many nationalities and cultures, and its baffling national character, was really impenetrable. So many astute observers of the human condition had made prize fools of themselves in the attempt to describe the Russian situation. Perhaps the most famous of these unwilling dupes was the 'Red Dean', the Rev. Hewlett Johnson, who said, after a visit in the 1930s, at the height of the purges when the population lived in a state of constant dread, 'What strikes the visitor most strongly is the complete absence of fear.' Even George Bernard Shaw was taken in: after visiting a Soviet prison, he pronounced it 'more humane than most British factories'.

Clearly what was needed was the evidence of people who had grown up in the Soviet system. Akhmatova and Mandelstam were witnesses whose evidence was certainly credible. Both were already established poets by the time of the revolution; they had refused, unlike many of their friends, to flee Russia, believing that they had a duty to stay and bear witness to the terrible events which had overtaken their country.

Akhmatova expressed her decision to reject the option of exile in these lines:

> I heard a voice call consolingly
> It was saying, come to me here,
> Leave your remote and sinful country,
> Leave Russia behind for ever.
> I will wash your hands of blood,
> Take the black shame from your heart,
> And cover up with another name
> The pain of insulting defeat.
> But with indifference, peacefully,
> I covered my ears with my palms,
> So that these unworthy words
> Should not sully my mournful spirit.

At the time of the Russian revolution, Akhmatova was 28. She was the daughter of a well-to-do family named Gorenko who considered her literary activities (she had published poems by the age of seventeen) as only suited to people of humble origin who could make a name for themselves by no other means. Her father persuaded her to publish pseudonymously and she adopted the name of Akhmatova, which reflected her mother's descent from the last Khan of the Golden Horde. (Having Tartar origins was not popular either, then or now.) Akhmatova was a beautiful girl, tall, slim, dark haired, fair skinned with pale grey-green eyes like those of a snow leopard. She was much sought after as a model by photographers and artists, including Modigliani.

The Bolsheviks, however, regarded Akhmatova as a symbol of the bourgeois culture they despised and which their revolution set out to destroy. (They were quite wrong – unlike most of her contemporaries, for example, she avoided the *avant-garde* in her verse.) She was thought to be an anachronism, unsuited to the harshness of the new steel age. (In this respect they were right. 'Why, there is nothing in her work except love, nothing about labour, or the collective,' wrote a Party hack. 'She cannot call our women into active participation and construction – only to God with his dear little angels.') But one woman prominent in the early communist regime, Alexandra Kollontay (later Soviet ambassador to Sweden and the first-ever female to hold such a post) saw in Akhmatova's poetry a strong espousal of the right of women to be regarded as individuals and not merely as sex objects. Now Akhmatova is seen by Soviet women as an important feminist.

To describe Akhmatova's life as harsh is to devalue language. Her first husband, the poet Nikolai Gumilyov, was shot in 1921 (Lenin knew of his arrest); her second husband, the art historian Nikolai Punin, died in prison. The regime did not know what to do with her – so she was simply given an old age pension, a mere pittance which kept her in cigarettes and tea. But she did retain the right to live in Leningrad and to visit Moscow, a right denied to most of her few surviving friends. She continued to produce poetry, much of it of a very fine quality, metrical, economical, lyrical and loving. But it was rarely written – words on paper were dangerous. Her poems (like those of Mandelstam) were memorized by herself and a few chosen friends.

Existing on black bread and sugarless tea, Akhmatova spent much of her time in bed, because of weakness and hunger. But she would often struggle to the jail where her son had been imprisoned for eighteen months as a means of maintaining a hold over her. (Akhmatova's desperation over her son's fate – she knew that one false step by her would be the end of him – foreshadowed the anguish of the mothers of the 'disappeared ones' in Argentina and elsewhere today.) In an effort to placate the regime, she wrote some doggerel verses in praise of Stalin which were published by the state publishing authorities in 1950. Once, while standing in line outside the prison in Leningrad, in the hope of seeing her son, she was recognized by 'a woman with blue lips standing behind me who of course had never heard my name. Suddenly, awakening from the benumbed condition in which we all found ourselves, she whispered in my ear – in those days, we all spoke in whispers – "Can you put this into words?" and I said, "I can." Something resembling a smile slipped over what had once been her face.'

The cycle of poems in which Akhmatova describes the suffering of this period begins:

> No, not beneath a foreign sky,
> Not sheltered by a foreign wing,
> I was where my people were,
> Where alas they were doomed to be.

In 1940, suddenly and inexplicably, permission was given for the publication of a volume of Akhmatova's poetry. Boris Pasternak* wrote to her that on the day of publication, despite people's tribulations, long queues formed in Moscow and the edition of 25,000 copies sold out quickly. However, a few months later the book was ordered to be removed from all libraries; this was due to direct intervention by Stalin, who, despite the war, still found time to worry about poets. No further publication was permitted. Someone had blundered in allowing the publication in the first place.

In *Hope against Hope*, Nadia Mandelstam tells the story of her husband's life and work and her own, with simplicity, dignity and a moving lack of self-pity. Osip Mandelstam is now widely regarded as the finest lyric poet Russia has produced in this century.† Although Mandelstam was personally timid, he had a tendency to be outspoken and sardonic in his writings. These were not characteristics which enhanced one's chance of survival in

---

* Pasternak was one of the few people Stalin actually liked as well as respected. This probably explains why he survived the purges of the thirties. But when *Dr Zhivago* was published in the West in 1957, and he was awarded the Nobel Prize, Pasternak was made *persona non grata*. Recently, however, there has been a move to rehabilitate him, to make his house a memorial and even to publish *Dr Zhivago* in Russia.

† This is the view of Sir Isaiah Berlin, an authority on Russian literature, and of Joseph Brodsky, perhaps Russia's best known modern poet, now in exile in the USA.

Stalin's Russia. After witnessing the terrible catastrophe which followed the forced collectivization of agriculture when millions of peasants and others perished from starvation, he foolishly composed a poem which he recited in Pasternak's apartment to an audience of ten friends – as he believed them to be. It said, in part:

> We live deaf to the land beneath us,
> Ten steps away, no one hears our speeches,
> All we hear is the Kremlin mountaineer,
> The murderer and peasant slayer.

Later Mandelstam altered the last two lines to something less libellous (and certainly less poetic):

> When there is so much as half a conversation,
> The Kremlin's mountaineer will get his mention.

But it was too late. Mandelstam had been denounced by one of his 'friends', as became apparent when the secret police quoted the dreadful first version to him. Nadia Mandelstam describes the night of her husband's arrest in this passage:

> Whenever Akhmatova came to visit us, she stayed in our tiny kitchen while I cooked our semblance of dinner on a kerosene stove in the corridor. In honour of our guest, I covered the gas cooker (the gas had not been connected) with an oil cloth to disguise it as a table. We called the kitchen our sanctuary after a visitor, looking in, said to Akhmatova – 'What are you doing here like a pagan idol in a sanctuary? Why don't you go to some meeting where you can at least sit down properly?' We had taken refuge there leaving Mandelstam to the mercy of the poetry-loving Brodsky.*

---

* David Brodsky (not to be confused with Joseph Brodsky, the poet), although a 'friend' of Mandelstam's, was in fact acting on instructions from the secret police to act as a witness to Mandelstam's arrest which was planned for later that night. All such arrests were made in the early hours which added greatly to people's fear. Despite their arbitrary and illegal nature, arrests had to be witnessed by two citizens, like the arrests by the Committee of Public Safety during the French Revolution.

In order to justify his prolonged visit, Brodsky had entertained Mandelstam by reciting poetry. The latter, wishing to be hospitable, had gone to a neighbour and scrounged an egg.

Suddenly, at 1 o'clock in the morning there was a sharp unbearably explicit knock on the door.

'They've come for Osip,' I said, and went to open the door.

At the time of his arrest, Mandelstam's manuscripts were bundled into sacks and taken to police headquarters. His wife commented: 'What do they do, in the bowels of our halls of justice, with all the papers, which in the early days, they took away in brief cases and now in sacks? But why speculate about the fate of papers when we don't know what happened to their owners?'

Nadia described the unimaginable scale of arrests during the thirties as follows:

The secret police did work to some sort of system. The object was to eradicate anyone with any spark of originality. People were picked up wholesale according to categories – churchmen, unbelievers, mystics, idealists, philosophers, humourists, people who talked too much, people who talked too little, people without humour, people with their own ideas about law, government and economics. To cover up blunders and failures, the concept of 'sabotage' was quickly introduced and on this pretext, engineers, technicians and any form of specialist could be and were arrested.

'Don't wear that hat,' Mandelstam once advised a fellow. poet. 'You mustn't draw attention to yourself or you will have trouble.'

The fact that Mandelstam was exiled to Voronezh and not shot out of hand was due largely to the intervention of his friend and admirer, Bukharin.*

* Bukharin, an original and important Bolshevik, was tried in 1938 for crimes including counter-revolutionary activity and complicity in 'Trotskyist' plots. Some of the accusations against him were ridiculous (for example, that he planned to turn Uzbekistan into a British colony). Bukharin defended himself vigorously, although confessing that he opposed Stalin because he believed Stalin's policies, especially the forced collectivization of agriculture, to be wrong. He knew that this confession would inevitably lead to a death penalty. He was correct. Bukharin's inexplicable confessions have never been explained. They certainly were not obtained by brain washing, torture or drugs. A reporter from the *Daily Telegraph* who witnessed the trial, when asked for a comment, replied: 'Everything is believable except the facts.'

'He hasn't done anything rash, has he?' Bukharin asked Nadia. 'No,' she replied. 'Only a few poems in his usual manner.'

Nadia claims that this lie weighed heavily on her conscience, but without it Mandelstam would have been doomed. Nevertheless, when Bukharin learned the truth he severed his connection with them. Nadia comments further:

> Is it alright to lie in order to save someone? Is it good to live in conditions where one does not have to lie? Do such conditions exist anywhere? We were brought up to believe that lying and hypocrisy is universal. I would certainly not have survived in our terrible times without lying. I have lied all my life: to my students, colleagues and even the good friends I didn't quite trust [this was true of most of them]. In the same way, no one trusted me.

Before Mandelstam's fate was known, Nadia rang a friend in the secret police seeking information.

'Let's hope they don't drive him out of his mind,' said her contact. 'Our fellows are very good at it.'*

A revealing glimpse of the way in which the Soviet system operated at this time is given by the letter Bukharin wrote to Stalin on behalf of Mandelstam. In a postscript, Bukharin mentioned that he had been visited by Boris Pasternak who was upset by the Mandelstam case. This was really an oblique way of referring to the opinion of literary circles. It was possible to mention an individual being upset, but unthinkable to mention the existence of dissatisfaction amongst a group in the community.

As a consequence of Bukharin's letter, Stalin actually rang Pasternak to discuss the matter. First he reproached Pasternak for not doing more to help his friend, then he asked:

'He's a genius, isn't he?'

'That's not the point,' Pasternak replied, avoiding an answer.

'What is it then?' Stalin asked.

Pasternak said that he would like to have a meeting when they could talk.

'What about?' Stalin responded.

---

* In the end, persecution drove Mandelstam mad.

'About life and death,' came the reply. Stalin hung up. Pasternak believed that if he had agreed that Mandelstam was a genius, which was indeed his opinion, the outcome would have been a death sentence. The news of this conversation created a state of short-lived ecstasy in literary circles, a feeling that they were ruled by a compassionate man concerned about the fate of poets.*

Mandelstam, however, realized that his exile was only a respite. He referred ironically to his situation in the following poem:

> Much we have to fear, big mouth beside me,
> Our tobacco turns to dust,
> Nut cracker, friend, idiot!
> I could have whistled through life like a starling,
> Eating nut pies.
> But clearly there's no chance of that.

At the height of his suffering, totally destitute, living in hunger and cold, he was able to write:

> Opulent poverty, regal indigence,
> Live in it calmly, be at peace,
> Blessed are these days, these nights,
> And innocent is the labour's singing sweetness.

The labour, of course, was his life's work, poetry.

By 1938, Mandelstam, in exile in Siberia, was out of his mind with fear; he suspected that his food was poisoned and would eat

---

* The regime continues to be hyper-sensitive to poets with awkward views; the savage twelve year sentence imposed on Irina Ratushinskaya is an example. This young poet, descended from the Polish aristocracy, wrote verse with a nationalistic fervour which angered the regime whose harsh treatment of her aroused worldwide condemnation. She was finally released with other high profile dissidents such as Orlov and Sakharov in late 1986. Despite her years of privation in prison and camps and the severe damage done to her health in consequence, Ratushinskaya has emerged with her trenchant views of Soviet society apparently unaffected. She has made a public statement that her release (and that of other well-known dissidents) should not deceive the West into believing that there has been a real change in Soviet policy. It would be naive for the West to believe the USSR was becoming more democratic. It remained an 'unhealthy society afflicted with the disease of totalitarianism'. She claims that there are at least 4000 political prisoners in the USSR. And while this situation persists, the West would be making a great mistake to place any trust in the Soviet leadership. She accused Gorbachev of mounting a campaign of deceit to attempt to improve trust, saying only the release of all political prisoners could begin to achieve this.

only half, after someone else had eaten the other half. In the end, he refused all food and lived from what he could scrounge. It is thought that his delusions led to him being thrown out of his hut into the snow and that he died of exposure. No one really knows, few care. The only information Nadia received was via a parcel she had sent her husband which was returned marked 'Addressee dead'.

In a second volume of memoirs,* Nadia explains the meaning of her husband's life, his work, his defiance and ultimate self-immolation in terms of the 'inner freedom' which was the basis of his values. In Stalin's Russia, this could be readily achieved by death.† Nadezhda Mandelstam herself exhibits the same inner spirit. She was 65 when she wrote *Hope Against Hope*, surely one of the great literary documents of the twentieth century. How can a woman survive such a life of deprivation and suffering with her sanity, integrity and eloquence intact? Joseph Brodsky, perhaps Russia's greatest modern poet, says that by absorbing all of Mandelstam's poetry, which she memorized, and much of Akhmatova's also, she absorbed their metricality, insight and intensity. That she was a difficult woman is attested by many of her friends who apparently resented the fame she had acquired through her husband's reflected glory – though it is more likely that they feared her relentless denunciation of the many members of the literary set who collaborated with the regime. She criticizes many people, sometimes without justification, but more often with ample reason. And she, in turn, has been accused of being unfair, capricious, intolerant, cranky, disagreeable and idiosyncratic. Perhaps she was all of these things; but from all accounts, so was Tolstoy.

In October 1938, Nadia wrote a letter to her husband which she reproduced as an epilogue to her memoirs:

Osia my beloved far away sweetheart, I have no words, my darling, to write in this letter which you may never read. I am sending it into empty space [in fact she never sent it, as she

* *Hope Abandoned*. Collins Harvill Press. 1974.

† Vladimir Bukovsky also uses the term 'inner freedom' to describe the weapon which some prisoners possessed which enabled them to withstand the greatest brutality and to defy their jailers.

had a presentiment that he was already dead]. Perhaps you will come back and not find me here. [Nadia lived precariously at this time as an English teacher in remote areas.] This will be all that is left for you to remember me by.

Osia, what a joy it was living together like children – all our squabbles and arguments, the games we played in our love. Now I don't even look at the sky – if I see a cloud, to whom can I show it? Remember the way we brought back provisions to make our poor feasts in the places where we pitched our tent like nomads? Remember the good taste of bread (when we got it by some miracle) and ate it together? And our last winter in Voronezh, our happy poverty and the poetry you wrote. [The Mandelstams' life in exile in Voronezh was indescribably hard as they had virtually no means of subsistence. But compared with what came later, it seemed like a time of delirious happiness.] I remember the time we were coming back from the baths and we bought some eggs and sausage. It was cold and I was freezing in my short jacket but nothing like what you must suffer now. I know how cold you are. That day comes back to me now – I understand so clearly, and ache from the pain of it, that those winter days, with all their troubles, were the greatest and the last days of happiness to be granted us.

My every thought is about you, my every tear and smile is for you. I bless every day and every hour of our bitter life together, my sweetheart, my companion, my blind guide in life. You are with me always, and I, who was so wild and angry, and never learnt to weep simple tears – now I weep and weep and weep.

It's me, Nadia. Where are you? Farewell.

CHAPTER 3

THE UNBREAKABLE BUKOVSKY

Early in 1975, the English actor David Markham* asked me to assist him in a campaign on behalf of a young Soviet dissident, Vladimir Bukovsky. By this time I had come to suspect that the human rights problem in the USSR was far worse than I had previously realized and that I could not stand aside should any opportunity present itself to do something about it. Markham had already pursued the Bukovsky case for six years with the same single-minded dedication as Rosemary Winckley had devoted to that of the Panovs, and had formed a committee which included Peggy Ashcroft, Iris Murdoch, Peter Hall, and Harold Pinter. After reading the file of documents on Bukovsky which he had compiled, I readily agreed to become involved in the campaign.

Bukovsky, then aged 34, had spent thirteen years in prison and special psychiatric 'hospitals'. He had, I gathered, been a rebellious student who, early in his life, became outspokenly critical of the Soviet regime. Bukovsky himself described the origins of his misfortunes thus:

I was seventeen and in the last year of school in Moscow. I started a little school magazine. It was done on a typewriter and consisted mainly of schoolboy jokes about the school and the teachers. There was a touch of schoolboy irony and parody but nothing political, and there was only one copy. We used to get together and read it to one another. Then, suddenly, there was an amazing reaction from the authorities. Dozens of officials started descending on us, from the Communist Party, and from the Ministry of Education. They set up committees of investigation and the result was that I was

---

* He died 17 December 1983.

expelled, the head master was dismissed and my father, a loyal Party member, received an official reprimand.

In 1961, Bukovsky enrolled as a student of bio-physics at Moscow University but was expelled after one term because of his involvement in an unofficial literary journal called *Phoenix* and for participating in poetry readings in Mayakovsky Square, a favourite spot for the recitation of 'dissident' poetry – Mayakovsky, a great Russian poet, had been an enthusiastic supporter of the revolution but a few years on and he committed suicide in despair. Following his expulsion, Bukovsky organized an exhibition of unofficial (i.e. *avant-garde*) art. After taking part in a geological expedition he finally took a conventional job as a programmer at the Moscow Cybernetics Centre.

Then, in 1963, he was arrested and charged with possessing two photocopies of *The New Class*.* Bukovsky was sent to the Serbsky Institute of Forensic Psychiatry† and, after an examination by a commission of psychiatrists, declared 'unaccountable for his actions' – i.e. insane. He was then admitted to the Leningrad 'Special' Psychiatric Hospital‡ where he spent fifteen months 'of

---

* This book by the former Vice President of Jugoslavia, Milovan Djilas, at one time Tito's heir apparent, was the first authoritative description of how the party officials and bureaucrats in communist countries had become hyper-privileged and had assumed many of the worst characteristics of the capitalist ruling class. It was, naturally, anathema to orthodox communists who hate and fear heretics far more than non-believers, as I later discovered.

† The Serbsky Institute of Forensic Psychiatry was founded in 1921. Its first director Vladimir Serbsky, who succeeded the eminent physician Sergei Korsakov as the state's leading authority on mental illness, allowed state ideology to permeate the Institute's functions, as happened in many branches of Soviet science at this time. Soon, the Serbsky simply became an arm of the state security system and acquired an evil reputation which it has not yet lost. It was to the Serbsky that intractable citizens – religious believers, nationalists, reformers, any sort of troublesome character – were sent. There they were assessed by doctors ready and willing to obey their real masters, the security chieftains. Once declared 'not responsible' by a compliant commission of psychiatrists, the victim could be deprived of liberty and of recourse to legal advice or help. He became a long-term, sometimes a permanent, prisoner of the state, disguised as a 'mentally ill person'. And he would remain in this situation until he recanted his views. Some victims remained prisoners for many years held in psychiatric hospitals under appalling conditions.

‡ 'Special' psychiatric hospitals in the USSR, as distinct from 'ordinary' ones, are under the control of the Ministry of the Interior KGB and not the Ministry of Health. Many of the doctors, as well as other staff, wear uniforms under their

hell'. He maintained his sanity during this period by teaching himself English.

After being released in December 1965, Bukovsky helped organize a demonstration in Pushkin Square, which had become a popular place for peaceful protests after the liberalization instigated by Khrushchev. The protestors were demanding the implementation of the 'rule of law' and access to the trial of Daniel and Sinyavsky – a *cause célèbre* which was attracting worldwide attention to the human rights problem in the USSR at the time (see Chapter 7). The demand that the regime respect the laws set out in the constitution was then, and still is, a central feature of the human rights movement in the USSR. Officially, the Soviet constitution guarantees many rights to its citizens, including the right to march peacefully in the streets, to meet together (but not secretly), to discuss grievances, and to express criticism of the government provided it is factual. But nothing which is 'against socialism' is legal, and, as the authorities are the sole judge of what this means, they can in practice suppress any activity of which they disapprove. The Soviet population know the effects of this catch-all provision from bitter experience and are inclined to look on those who choose to ignore it as 'crazy', or at least, very deficient in the instinct of self-preservation.

In fact, Bukovsky never participated in the actual demonstration over Daniel and Sinyavsky, having been re-incarcerated in a psychiatric hospital a few days before it took place. But he was soon released and immediately joined a demonstration in Pushkin Square protesting at the arrest of three 'dissidents', Alexander Ginzburg, Yuri Galanskov and Alexei Dobrovolsky, who were charged with 'violating public order' (their case is described later). As a result he was again arrested and this time sentenced to three years in a labour camp. In his final pleå at his trial he stated: 'Freedom of speech and of the press, which is our constitutional right, is, first of all, freedom to criticize. Nobody anywhere has ever forbidden praise of the government.' He declared that he

footnote continued

white coats. Apart from the incarceration of patients with genuine and dangerous mental illness, they are used for holding sane persons with awkward – i.e. 'dangerous' – views, dissidents. The regime can be quite terrifying and many former inmates say that the worst hard labour camps are comfortable, cosy places in comparison.

had committed no criminal act, that he did not regret his participation in the demonstration, and that, when he was free, 'I shall again organize demonstrations in complete conformity with the law – as before.'

Bukovsky served his full three years in a camp near Voronezh, and, soon after his release, in 1970, resumed his activities in defence of human rights. In an interview which was broadcast widely to the free world, he stated:

The essence of the struggle is the struggle against fear – the fear that has gripped the people since Stalin's time and which has still not left them. It is thanks to this fear that the present system of dictatorship and oppression continues to exist. In this struggle against fear, personal example is vital. The fact that I am still alive shows that it is possible to fight and survive.

During his brief period of freedom, Bukovsky was able to obtain details of a number of dissidents who, like himself, had been certified insane and held in penal psychiatric hospitals. The list included, Petr Grigorenko, Natalya Gorbanevskaya, Viktor Fainberg and Vladimir Borisov. These were all well-known human rights activists; they have since been exiled to the West and have been found after psychiatric examination to be sane.* Bukovsky obtained photocopies of the clinical documents relating to these cases and sent them to the West, requesting that they be examined by competent doctors and an opinion expressed as to whether the clinical facts justified the forcible exclusion of the subjects from contact with society. Most provocative from the Soviet standpoint was his request that, should his view that the clinical evidence indicated mental normality be corroborated, the facts should be transmitted to the appropriate authorities of the World Psychiatric Association to be considered at their Congress scheduled for the end of 1971 in Mexico City.

In response to this appeal, an Ad Hoc Working Group on the Internment of Dissenters in Mental Hospitals was set up in

---

* Over the years, I have met all of them, and although I am not a psychiatrist, I am an experienced physician and would, without hesitation, endorse the view that they are all sane.

London to examine Bukovsky's material in particular and the whole question of the political abuse of psychiatry in general. The Working Group comprised psychiatrists, other doctors and medical workers, human rights activists, and experts in Soviet affairs. Its findings were published in the London *Times* of 16 September 1971 together with the opinion of 44 psychiatrists, including most of the leading professors of psychiatry in Britain. Grave doubts were expressed about the treatment of those described in the Bukovsky papers; four were considered to have no symptoms, none were believed to require either hospitalization or any form of confinement on medical grounds.

The publication of the Bukovsky documents aroused worldwide indignation and, in retaliation, Bukovsky was re-arrested on a serious charge of 'anti-Soviet propaganda'. He was again sent to the Serbsky Institute but, in view of the publicity in the West which now surrounded his every action, he was pronounced 'accountable' for his actions (i.e. miraculously sane) and sent for trial.

The trial was rushed through in one day. Bukovsky was refused permission to call any witnesses, although several inmates of psychiatric hospitals were prepared to confirm in court the accuracy of his documents. No friend was admitted to this so called 'open trial' nor were any independent journalists. The judge did not allow any discussion of the crucial issue – whether Bukovsky's allegations 'were accurate and truthful' or not.

In his final address Bukovsky stated: 'Our society is still sick with the fear it inherited from Stalin's terror. But the process of regeneration has begun and there is no stopping it. I will continue the fight for legality and justice.' He was sentenced to two years in prison, five years in a strict regime camp and five years of exile for the crime of perpetrating 'slanderous inventions', i.e. arranging for the clinical notes of sane victims of psychiatric terror to be published abroad.

Although I had been dimly aware of the use of psychiatry as a means of disposing of awkward citizens in communist countries (it is not unknown in non-communist ones as the film *One Flew Over the Cuckoo's Nest* so graphically suggests), I believed it to involve only a few cases and to be mainly an expression of a very different social *milieu* with different values and concepts of normality. I also suspected that a major factor would prove to be the backwardness of Soviet medicine in general (of which I had had experience in my own speciality of heart disease) and of psychiatry in particular. On a visit to a leading cardiological institute in Moscow in 1968 I had seen evidence of a number of nineteenth-century practices and I suspected that the Soviet approach to psychiatric illness was probably equally primitive. I was soon disabused of this facile notion by further exposure to the facts.

Among the documents given me by David Markham was a *Manual of Psychiatry* composed by Bukovsky and a Ukrainian psychiatrist named Semyon Gluzman who, after writing a report highly critical of the diagnosis of mental illness in the cases of Petr Grigorenko and Leonid Plyushch (see Chapter 13), was himself sentenced to seven years' hard labour and three years of exile. Gluzman and Bukovsky became friends while serving in the same labour camp. The *Manual* contained advice for dissidents undergoing psychiatric examination and explained how best to prepare for the interrogation and to defend oneself against a false diagnosis of insanity.

The *Manual of Psychiatry* clearly described how Soviet psychiatrists were being taught to diagnose schizophrenia on the basis of a symptomatology which would not be accepted in any civilized country.* According to the *Manual*, a new category of illness called 'creeping schizophrenia' had been recognized in the USSR. Its victims did not, at least in the early stages, experience the hallucinations or delusions that are characteristic of schizophrenia. On the contrary, clinical normality was a feature of the 'disease'. The patients were, however, subject to pessimism and melancholia, inflexibility and stubbornness (common traits in Russians as anyone familiar with Russian literature will know) and, more significantly, they displayed a tendency to oppose authority, to reject tradition, and to question official policy – a state of mind described as 'reformist'. Other symptoms commonly found were strong religious convictions, an excessive view of one's own worth,

---

* It should, however, be added that schizophrenia is sometimes difficult to diagnose. There is no doubt that seriously disturbed patients who are a grave danger to society can appear 'normal' to their relatives and associates – there have been a number of multiple killers in this category, for example, Peter Sutcliffe, the 'Yorkshire Ripper'. Their mental abnormality may only become apparent after they have been caught committing a crime.

a tendency to attention seeking, and a strong desire to emigrate. The last was considered clear evidence of a delusional mental state – anyone who believed any other social system to be superior to socialism *must* be mad.

In short, the whole concept of 'creeping schizophrenia' was quite as ridiculous as Lysenko's genetic theories, but, like Lysenkoism, it had been accepted with relish and approval because it conformed to the ideology of the state. Ultimately, like Lysenkoism, it was to lead the Soviet Union into one of its greatest humiliations. The chief promoter of the concept was the leading psychiatrist and head of the Institute of Psychiatry of the Soviet Academy of Medical Sciences, Andrei Snezhnevsky. But although Snezhnevsky's views were widely adopted by Soviet psychiatrists, largely because it was soon perceived that they had the endorsement of the people at 'the top' and that resistance was therefore both futile and dangerous, it would be wrong to believe that they were universally accepted or acted upon. Opposition took many forms. One doctor, ordered by the KGB to admit a sane person as a patient, wrote 'practically normal' under 'diagnosis' and 'acting on orders from above' under 'reason for admission'. But the commonest form of resistance was the usual method in the USSR – pass the case on to 'higher authority' for decision.

It seemed to me, after reading this account of how perfectly normal behaviour characteristics could lead to a lifetime in a horrendous prison, that Orwell's worst fears were being exceeded. I could scarcely believe that this was happening on anything but a very small scale. I was disabused when David Markham arranged for me to meet Marina Voikhanskaya, a Soviet psychiatrist then living in London.

CHAPTER 4

SOME 'CREEPING SCHIZOPHRENICS'

Marina Voikhanskaya, an appealing woman with an almost English sense of irony, explained to me that she had become involved in the dissident movement while working in a psychiatric hospital in Leningrad where she had found a sane young patient who, she said, was dying of neglect and loneliness. None of the staff would have anything to do with him; he did not even have a toothbrush. His troubles had started after he had sent some *avant-garde* paintings to an exhibition in Paris. He was convicted of some trifling breach of the regulations and exiled for eight years. When allowed back into the world, he was forbidden to return to Leningrad and sent to Smolensk where he was ordered to work in a ceramic factory decorating pottery. After two years he fled to Moscow but was picked up by the KGB and put on a train to Leningrad. On arriving there, he was put on another train to Smolensk. He then spent the next two years shunting between the three cities. Finally he was put into the psychiatric hospital as an incorrigible, anti-social misfit. Because of the KGB's interest in the case, the staff neglected him – better not to be involved. Marina, undaunted, befriended him, visiting him every day and ensuring that he received proper attention. But her interest in this tragic patient attracted adverse comments from her colleagues and this increased her awareness of the inhumanity of the Soviet system. She then gravitated towards more advanced dissident activity.

When Marina persisted in her activities, she was given the choice of prison or exile. She chose to leave Russia although she knew this would be painful – like many dissidents, she had a great love of her country, it was the regime that she disliked. She was also forced to leave her eleven-year-old boy, Misha, behind. At the time of her departure, her divorced husband had promised not to hinder the emigration of the child but after Marina had left, and under pressure from the KGB, he withheld his consent to Misha's emigration. I visited the child in Leningrad where he was living with his grandmother; he was beautiful and clever, but very lonely, especially as he was ostracized at school. He consoled himself with loving a rather scraggy black cat. I left him a Meccano set which gave him something else to play with.

I kept my visit rather short fearing (needlessly) that there would be a brisk rap on the door at any moment. This didn't happen, largely, I believe, because the taxi I had hired turned out, by chance, to be an official limousine whose driver was earning a little money on the side – I had noticed that it was rather luxurious. If the driver had reported my visit to the police, he would also have had to explain his own activities.

Marina painted a dismal picture of the standard of Soviet hospital care – even small provincial hospitals in the UK, she said, were better equipped than many major Soviet ones. Over-crowding was rife, all medicines, even basic ones, were scarce or non-existent, there was a grave shortage of equipment and appliances and, above all, the medical service was permeated by a gross lack of concern for patients' welfare and by corruption. She had herself been a patient suffering a lung abscess as a complication of pneumonia. She said that she had to bribe the nurses to change her sheets more frequently than the regulation ten days, despite the drenching sweats which occur in such cases.*

On 27 November 1975 I went with David Markham to a meeting at Central Hall Westminster which had been arranged by Amnesty to protest at the repression of dissent in the USSR and especially the abuse of psychiatry and the continuing imprisonment of Bukovsky. As we entered the hall, we were booed by a crowd of demonstrators holding placards which proclaimed Amnesty International to be a CIA front. Ironically, this same day, Amnesty had issued a report detailing the corruption and brutality of the regime of the Shah of Iran and revealing that there were 25,000 political prisoners in that country being held without trial. I asked a jeering young girl in the picket line if she thought Bukovsky deserved to be in jail. She answered with one word – 'Yes.' God help Britain if people like this ever get political power, I thought.

The meeting was addressed by Leonid Plyushch, by now an

* There is now a crisis in the health of the Soviet population where, in men, the expectation of life has fallen to about 62 years compared to 72 years in the US. There are many factors involved, poor medical care being only one.

exile in Paris. Plyushch has been described by Bukovsky, with whom he shared a cell, as the bravest man he had ever met and *The Manual of Psychiatry for Dissenters* was dedicated to him. Plyushch, a mathematician, had resisted the brutal methods used by his jailers and had refused to recant his dissident views. He has an attractive spiritual quality and an undiminished commitment to human rights.

The maltreatment of Plyushch, so eminently sane, had aroused great indignation in France, especially amongst mathematicians and scientists, and in October 1975 a symposium organized by Amnesty which featured the Plyushch case had attracted an audience of 5000. The French Communist Party, aware of how much damage this brutality was doing to its electoral image, demanded his release, even threatening to break with Moscow on the issue. Plyushch and his family were sent into exile next day. After arriving in Austria, Plyushch gave a press conference; his testimony concerning his treatment contained this passage:

The horror of the madhouse gripped me from the start. In the wards, there were more patients than beds; I was put as the third person on two bunks pushed together. On the beds, patients were writhing from the effects of haloperidol [a strong psychotropic drug which often produces involuntary and painful muscular spasms]. One man's tongue was hanging out, another rolling his eyes. Another stumbled about bent over in a painful and unnatural position. Some patients lay groaning from the effects of sulfazine injections [a therapeutically useless and very painful drug administered as a punishment]. I saw that the purpose of the 'treatment' was to break the patient's spirit, first his will to resist, then any interest in political or social problems or his family. In the end, one became indifferent to everything except survival. I wanted to remember what they had done to me – in fact I remembered only a hundredth part of what I saw.

Another of the speakers at Central Hall was the Soviet dissident poet, Natalya Gorbanevskaya, who had come to the meeting from Paris where she lived as an exile. Natalya, small, soft, plump and cheerful, was one of the founders and an editor of the *Chronicle* *of Current Events*, a dissident publication* whose importance equalled that of Solzhenitsyn's *A Day in the Life of Ivan Denisovich*. It reported in simple, accurate detail everything that was known about dissident activity and a good deal else besides. It invariably claimed at its masthead that everything contained within was believed to be accurate but should anything prove to be wrong, a correction would be published in the next issue. This disclaimer was essential to conform to the Soviet constitution which permits critical comments provided they are true. The *Chronicle* was a *samizdat* publication – that is self-produced and unofficial. Typewritten copies were circulated by hand, further copies were made by the recipients and circulated like a chain letter. The *Chronicle* gave concrete reality to the slogan: 'No one is forgotten, nothing is forgotten'. It gave heart to many political prisoners who came to realize that it defended them against anonymity – was indeed their only real defence. For information from the *Chronicle* soon found its way to the West where it was often transmitted back to the USSR via the various foreign radio services, and thus widely circulated. The *Chronicle*'s editors and contributors, among whom were Valery Chalidze, exiled in 1972, and Pavel Litvinov, exiled in 1974, remained anonymous. Natalya's involvement only became public after she was charged with it as an offence.†

Natalya spoke for fifteen minutes in flawless English. It was only later, at a party, that I discovered that she did not in fact speak much English. She had written out her speech in Russian, had it translated into English and then memorized this text. Only a poet could do such a thing, I thought. I also learned something of her background – she had been a student of history and language at Moscow University but had fallen foul of the authorities after writing some sad love poems which were, she was told, 'degenerate' and 'pessimistic'. She was expelled from the University on the grounds that it was decadent for a socialist to be anything but optimistic. From 1955 onwards she began writing

---

* The *Chronicle* was published in English by Amnesty until it ceased to appear in 1982 after everyone associated with it had been arrested or blackmailed.

† In an interview with Michael Scammell published in *Index* she stated that the fact that her friends entrusted the *Chronicle* to her made it the most important of her life's works.

serious poetry which was published in *samizdat* form. The frequent re-typing* of her poems, the only method of distribution,
led to many errors and after a while she would have to recall them
and make corrections.

In 1968, Natalya took part in a demonstration in Pushkin Square
against the Soviet invasion of Czechoslovakia. She was arrested
with the other demonstrators, subjected to a psychiatric examination by a commission of three doctors, pronounced 'not responsible' but allowed to go home because she had two small children
to care for. But later she got into more trouble and finished up in
a psychiatric hospital for two years.

My discussions with Plyushch and Gorbanevskaya removed
most of my doubts about the accuracy of the accusation that
psychiatry was being used as a political weapon in the USSR. I
concluded that, as a doctor, I couldn't stand by and do nothing; I
became a member of the Working Group on the Internment of
Dissenters in Mental Hospitals and, in 1982, I succeeded Peter
Reddaway as its Chairman.

It might be thought that, as a non-psychiatric physician, I would
have difficulty in fulfilling a useful role, but my lack of psychiatric
qualifications proved to be no handicap. Most of the other medical
members were fully trained psychiatrists and it was from them
that any specialist decisions stemmed. My role was mainly to
coordinate, administrate and initiate action. I soon found that
there were many difficulties. Psychiatry is uniquely vulnerable to
attack from many quarters and, as a result, and not unnaturally,
very defensive. The criteria of mental illness are subjective and
many extraneous factors enter the picture – culture, language,
tradition, customs, rites, taboos, to say nothing of economic and
social factors. The Japanese approach to mental illness, for
example, is very different to that of the British and, in many
respects, would be regarded in Britain as repressive.

A major bugbear is the difficulty of making a clear distinction
between medical malpractice and abuse. The former is common

---

* All photocopying apparatus is under strict supervision in the USSR. Every
photocopy must bear the stamp of the department in control of the apparatus. To
possess a photocopy made without authorization is a crime. The authorities are
now finding that to try to control the spread of information in the midst of an
information revolution is to create an insuperable obstacle to progress.

in all countries – but it is sporadic and does not have a political intent (that, at least, is generally the rule, although there are undoubtedly exceptions). One of our difficulties was to justify (which we could not) the fact that so many inmates of British prisons are clearly mentally ill and in need of psychiatric care rather than custodial sentences. The widespread use of tranquillizing drugs and anti-depressants in British prisons, often administered by doctors not well-trained in their use, is notorious. There were also disturbing reports (later confirmed) of psychiatric patients being brutalized by warders at hospitals such as Rampton. The Soviets were well aware of these scandals and countered our accusations with their own; and in the case of the US they could point to even greater and more impressive abuses. But without diminishing the importance of these problems, they are different to the question of the deliberate use by state authority of psychiatry as a means of suppressing dissent.

CHAPTER 5

CONVERSATIONS WITH IVY

It was soon after the Amnesty meeting at Central Hall, that I first met Tanya, the daughter of Maxim Litvinov, and her daughters, Masha (now Lady Phillimore) and Vera, the separated wife of Valery Chalidze, who, with Andrei Sakharov, was the co-founder of the Human Rights Committee in Moscow. I came to know and like them very well, as, I soon discovered, did many other people.

The Litvinov family brought to the dissident movement a strong liberal influence inherited from Ivy, Tanya's English mother. I met Ivy several weeks later; she lived near Brighton with Tanya and I made a number of journeys with Masha, Vera and their children to visit them. The account which follows is based on the notes I made of my conversations with Ivy.

Ivy met Maxim Litvinov, a young Bolshevik living in exile in London, in 1916, while browsing in a Hampstead book shop. She took an immediate interest in this strange young man, almost unique in that he was not in uniform. There were, as she wrily observed, few other men available at the time. She contrived a formal introduction, fell in love, got pregnant and married. She faced fierce parental opposition; but Ivy had a strong will which she presumably inherited from her own mother, who was the daughter of a colonel in the Indian Army. From her father, who was an educationalist of some note, she inherited a life-long love of literature. She told me that years later the only thing that made her life in Moscow tolerable was the access she was given to Stalin's library which was apparently extensive, but not used by its owner. She also established a friendship, of a rather intimate nature she hinted, with James Joyce during one of her husband's frequent official visits to Paris. Of politics she knew nothing and cared less. She said she had never heard of Karl Marx until Maxim spoke of him. She added that Litvinov derided Marxism and, after a few months' practical experience of it, communism also. When the war was over, by which time Ivy already had two children, a son, Michael, and a daughter, Tanya, Maxim Litvinov was returned to Russia in exchange for Sir Robert Bruce Lockhart. Her family told Ivy that she would never see him again; but, to their chagrin, he sent for her, and despite the turbulence of Russia and the xenophobia of a regime then fighting for its life against the interventionist armies, Ivy went. She lived in Russia for fifty years but never lost her imperious English manner or accent.

Litvinov was appointed deputy to Chicherin, the first Soviet Commissar for Foreign Affairs. Ivy spoke with relish of the time that Chicherin, a homosexual, had his trousers stolen while having an illicit affair. (Homosexuality was then, as now, a serious criminal offence in the USSR.) As there were no other trousers immediately available, a delicate situation developed. How it was resolved I never discovered. By the early thirties, Litvinov had risen to the position of Commissar for Foreign Affairs. He was widely admired in the West – possibly the only high Soviet official to be so. He was also one of the few original Bolsheviks to die in his bed of natural causes. He never knew why he survived the purges, but Ivy believed that even after he was replaced as Foreign Minister by Molotov in preparation for the pact with Hitler, Stalin wished to preserve the one man who remained *persona grata* with western leaders, in case of future need. Stalin's trust in Hitler's pledges was less than unshakeable.

In the thirties, Litvinov strove for real disarmament and when this policy failed, he tried to forge an alliance with France and Britain against fascism. He preached the simple slogan, true today as it was then, that 'peace is indivisible'. When Hitler invaded Russia, Litvinov was sent to Washington to be Soviet Ambassador and Ivy believed that his warm, humanistic personality played an important part in persuading Roosevelt, incorrectly, that the Russian bear was tameable.

In 1944, when it was clear that fascism was going to be defeated, Litvinov was recalled to Moscow. He now opposed Stalin vigorously, arguing that Soviet efforts to seek security through the domination of Eastern Europe would destroy all the goodwill built up during the war and would lead, in the end, to endless conflict with the West. He advocated a policy of cooperation and moderation in international affairs. Stalin listened but chose to ignore this excellent advice.

Although Litvinov's services to Russia were invaluable, this never endeared him (or anyone else) to Stalin, said Ivy. Her husband lived in constant fear of the door bell; he stayed up till very late every night playing bridge because he had a horror of being taken from his warm bed to be executed. From time to time the bridge game would be interrupted while the players listened in dread to the noise of other occupants of their apartment block being arrested. When, in the very early hours, Litvinov was persuaded to go to bed, he slept with a revolver under his pillow. Ivy was instructed to knock on his door in a special way if the police came for him, so giving him enough time to commit suicide. (On a visit to Moscow I was shown the room where Litvinov enacted this nightly drama by members of his family who still live in the apartment.) Once, Ivy said, she gave the coded knock accidentally, but realized what she had done just in time to prevent Maxim from shooting himself.

Stalin did not fraternize with his officials and Ivy met him only rarely. But once he appeared, unexpectedly, at a lunch Litvinov was giving for the Finnish ambassador to celebrate the conclusion of a treaty. Stalin shook hands with Ivy who was seated next to the ambassador and spoke to her warmly, mistaking her for the ambassador's wife. 'Stalin was such a peasant,' commented Ivy, 'he didn't know that wives sat opposite their husbands at official dinners.'

Ivy's views on the human rights question were of special interest to me. She said that her husband grew to detest communism because of its inhumanity and that so did most of the other leading communists. She was scathing about President Carter's professed aim of making human rights a central policy issue between the USA and the USSR because it had come much too late. She felt that the non-communist powers should have insisted on a proper respect for human rights from the start and that the Soviet Union should never have been admitted to the League of Nations nor given economic and technical aid by America until it agreed to respect ordinary legality and, above all, to give its citizens freedom from arbitrary arrest. She felt that unfreedom was now so firmly established in the Soviet system that it could never be reversed. She did not believe that the dissident movement, in which her children and grandchildren were very involved, would change things. The bureaucrats realized that lack of freedom hampered the development of the country but they feared change more than they regretted stagnation.

Finally, said Ivy, her husband had been constantly amazed at the gullibility and weakness of the leaders of Britain, France and America in the thirties. They allowed any bluff from the dictators, no matter how transparent, to succeed, and had given way to any demand, no matter how outrageous. Stalin used to laugh about it. Some twenty years after Litvinov's death, Ivy, who had retained her British passport, was allowed to return to Britain. Her daughter was allowed to join her, at first for a visit; later, however, Tanya decided not to return to Russia. Tanya's daughters, Masha and Vera, were permitted to emigrate after Henry Kissinger interceded actively on their behalf with the Soviet Foreign Ministry.

CHAPTER 6

GLIMPSES OF SOVIET REALITY

In the months which followed my first meeting with Tanya and her daughters, I had numerous discussions with them, and it was from these that I obtained the most vivid, and I believe, the most authentic picture of contemporary Soviet life. Although they had lived as the children and grandchildren of a privileged Soviet leader and belonged to a well-educated postwar generation, Masha and Vera still found much to disapprove of and to oppose. They could only be called dissidents in the sense that William Wilberforce was a dissident. They had never sought to subvert the Soviet system, only to humanize it. ('Is this possible?' I wrote in my diary. 'I hope so. If not, there will ultimately be a catastrophe.')

Tanya Litvinov is charming and, like her mother and daughters, highly intelligent, but she is also self-effacing, and maintains that her role in the dissident movement had never been important. It was only after I had met many of her old friends, both in the Soviet Union and in the emigré community, that I discovered just how valuable a contribution she had made.* Tanya was in fact one of the most stalwart defenders of human rights in Russia, although she had managed to maintain a low profile. Among her many interesting comments I found particularly enlightening her views of Akhmatova, whom she had known well, and Nadia Mandelstam. She claimed that Nadia Mandelstam was a rather disagreeable woman who made life unpleasant for her husband and was now basking in his reflected glory. She admitted, however, that Nadia's feat of remembering Mandelstam's poetry was very important and that without her, most of it would have been lost. I would quickly discover that Soviet emigrés were prone to denigrate each other. Alexander Zinoviev claims that Russians

* On her visit to London in May 1986, to see Mrs Thatcher, Elena Bonner the wife of Andrei Sakharov insisted that time had to be found for a meeting with Tanya Litvinov if no one else.

have made denunciation of each other into an art form. It is, in a sense, a manifestation of the type of affection mixed with envy which shared catastrophe breeds. In any case, writers do not have to be likeable to be credible.

Tanya said she finally decided not to return to Russia (she still had a passport, unlike her daughters) after enrolling in a drawing class run by the Brighton Borough Council. The enrolment procedure took half an hour and enabled her to indulge a life-long wish to study drawing. In Russia, she explained, she would have had to apply for permission to a committee at her place of work, and, provided it had been approved (and if it had not been approved, no reasons would have been given her), the application would have wended its way through various committees each of which could have withheld approval at will. The process of getting approval (or being denied it) might have taken two years, by which time she would probably have lost interest in the project. The ease of getting permission to learn to draw in England, brought home to her (as did other experiences) just how restrictive and oppressive life in Russia really was. She decided she could not face any more of it and that she wanted to remain in England. She told me that the most used word in Russia was 'permission'. Someone's permission was required for virtually every course of action in life and, to add to the frustration, permission was granted or withheld capriciously. No one was accountable, errors or injustice could not be corrected except by a tortuous and uncertain process which could often lead to further trouble and disappointment.

The picture of Soviet life which Vera and Masha painted coincided in many ways with descriptions I had been given by Marina and other emigrés. Life for the ordinary person was, they said, so harassing that people only survived as in a shipwreck, by a resolute camaraderie. The nervous toll, however, was high, and the general mood of the people was one of irritability and impatience. Greatly adding to people's frustration and irritability were the strains imposed by having to have both husband and wife working in order to cover basic living costs and the never decreasing gap between expectations (which are always rising) and the possibilities of fulfilment (which are not). Socialist man has proved, contrary to prediction, to be as greedy, avaricious and self-centred as any other – as anyone with a simple grasp of human nature might reasonably have expected to be the case.

An equally revealing, and even more current, picture of what was happening to the mood and morale of the educated classes of the Soviet Union in the late 1970s was given me by Valentin Turchin at a private meeting we had after his visit to the Institute of Physics to discuss the continued exile of Yuri Orlov. I had first met this most intelligent and engaging of men, a leading Soviet mathematician and computer analyst, in Moscow in 1977, at a party with Mrs Orlov and a number of other dissidents. Valentin was a founder of the Amnesty International group in Moscow and was soon forced to go abroad. Himself a member of the 'new technocracy', whose numbers are already large, and grow daily larger, he explained the attitudes of its members in a way that I found wholly credible.

Education and ever-expanding technology has inevitably produced a new class of technocrats in the USSR, just as in every industrialized country. The previous generation of technocrats were described dismissively by Nadia Mandelstam as fully contented with their lot. They had had more than enough of turmoil – all they wanted was an apartment, a car, holidays on the Black Sea and the freedom to attend to their computers in peace. But the younger generation inevitably had higher aspirations, Turchin explained, and as most of these aspirations were to be frustrated by bureaucratic interference, it was inevitable that the growing ranks of the dissident movement would contain a high proportion of scientists and technologically trained people. This was new: historically, reformers in Russia have always come from a literary background.

The keynotes of modern science are first, its universality and, second, the ever-increasing speed of change. Every first-class scientist needs to keep closely in touch with the developments in his field and this can only be done by frequent and unfettered communication with his peers whoever and wherever they are. Modern scientific communication depends increasingly on international meetings of fellow workers. It is simply not possible to keep abreast by reliance on scientific publications, even if these are made freely available which, in the USSR, they are not. The desire to participate in international meetings has several adverse effects on scientists in the USSR. First, the only hope they have of getting permission, and this is often a very capricious decision, is to be regarded as ideologically thoroughly reliable. Zhores Medvedev told me once, when we were discussing the Soviet psychiatrist Marat Vartanian, the assistant director of the Moscow Psychiatric Research Institute who seems to turn up at every international meeting in his field, that this makes it highly probable that he is not only trusted by the KGB but probably an officer in it. I imagine his wife has a collection of fur coats even a film star might envy.

But ideological reliability does not usually go together with scientific excellence – quite the contrary. It is the enquiring, sceptical mind which is most likely to find the hidden clues in science as in every other field of human thought. This would not be an attribute likely to endear its possessor to authority or to produce permission to travel abroad – quite the contrary.

This problem does not begin or end with scientists. Education generally must breed enquiry and doubt. The dogmas of the past must come under increasing scrutiny and when, as is now happening, the dogmas are seen to contain many errors, then the questions start. Thus the ranks of the dissidents increase. It is not the worker confronted with monotonous drudgery who seeks to challenge the system – his solution is the bottle of vodka which he is likely to consume at the end of his shift and at the factory gate. The spread of education has produced an ever-growing population of readers, viewers, and thinkers who are more intelligent and better informed than the official educational product which is served up to them. Increasingly they turn to unofficial (*samizdat*) sources of information. They listen avidly to the broadcasts from abroad (even when they are jammed), they do everything possible to meet and talk to visitors from abroad and, of course, they try, sometimes successfully, to get permission to travel abroad. Overseas travel soon reveals that life in the West bears little relation to the official version they are accustomed to receiving. As a result it has now become self-evident to a large section of the educated population of the Soviet Union that the official media have served up a sterilized version of Soviet life for much too long. Since the accession of Mikhail Gorbachev there has been a growing demand for more 'openness' – how far this will go remains to be seen.

CHAPTER 7

SOME RUSSIAN LITERARY CRITICS

Since the dissident activity in which the Litvinov family and their friends and relatives played so prominent a part largely revolved around a series of 'literary scandals' and trials, it seemed to me worth while to explore these matters in some detail and to try and understand the background to the drama. Writers have always had a special role in Russian life for, in the absence of democratic institutions, it is only they who can ask the questions and give expression to the agonies of the people. The Litvinov granddaughters grew up in the atmosphere of gradually increasing liberalization which followed the death of Stalin. But the process of liberalization soon faltered in the face of opposition from the entrenched bureaucracy which it threatened. After Khrushchev's frank admissions of Stalin's crimes at the 20th Congress of the Communist Party in 1956, there was a crack-down on dissident activity, especially that involving writers. This culminated in 1966 with the trial and conviction of two well-known writers, Yuli Daniel and Andrei Sinyavsky, whose importance in literary circles was symbolized by the fact that it was they who carried the lid of Pasternak's coffin at his funeral.

Sinyavsky and Daniel were the first important writers to be prosecuted and convicted since the death of Stalin and their trial was conducted with such flagrant disregard for legal norms – the 'evidence' being clearly manufactured and the courtroom packed with KGB operatives disguised as 'citizens' – that people at once perceived that the old Stalinist techniques were being resurrected. There was a storm of protest both at home and abroad; the regime was sending an unequivocal signal to the world, and the world was not willing to accept it without demur. The resulting protest revealed widespread anger, dismay and hostility; but it was quite unavailing.

The Litvinovs were soon caught up in the aftermath of these

events which, to some extent, still reverberate through the Soviet Union, and beyond.

In order to understand what happened it is necessary to start with Alexander Solzhenitsyn, whose work captured the imagination of the civilized world like that of no other writer since Tolstoy. His unique personal experiences of Russian life in all its complexity and tyranny, his intense patriotism and his religious fervour combine to make him an awesome figure. Zhores Medvedev says that the publication of *One Day in the Life of Ivan Denisovich* in 1962 marked a great change in the intellectual life of the Soviet Union. His own excitement on receiving an advance copy of the work was intense – he read it three times in succession. Apparently Khrushchev had it read to him by an attendant while on holiday and was so moved that he consulted his one loyal supporter, Mikoyan, who agreed that it should be published. This required a submission to the Central Committee Praesidium, for no other authority could override the censors. (Khrushchev had the power to forbid publication but not to permit something to be published against a ruling of the censors.)

The critical reception of the book in Russia was at first enthusiastic – *Pravda* likened its depiction of the Russian character to the finest passages of Tolstoy. There was widespread recognition that it combined honest realism (hitherto very rare in communist literature) with compassion and artistry. A million copies of the book were sold very rapidly.

But the deluge of manuscripts which subsequently flooded editorial offices with stories, essays, diaries and novels describing many aspects of life under Stalin – the camps, the convict trains, the prisons with their brutality and lawlessness, the purges, the liquidations, the widespread suffering of the population and many other painful subjects – frightened even Khrushchev. He rejected appeals to ease the censorship which had for so long ensured that all this anguish would remain secret; the writings were, he said, a stew 'that will attract flies like a carcass, enormous fat flies, all sorts of bourgeois scum from abroad will come crawling all over it'. When the hierarchy saw what it had done, it became even more nervous and the censorship was tightened further. Khrushchev was deposed in 1964 and his successor, Leonid Brezhnev, at once began to clean up all the 'liberal filth' his predecessor's unfortunate policies had unleashed on a population hitherto undefiled by exposure to the truth. The state publishing house refused to publish any more of Solzhenitsyn's books, especially *Cancer Ward* and *The First Circle*. (In an interview on American television, on 25 June 1974, Solzhenitsyn stated that he had been told by the Soviet authorities that *Cancer Ward* would be published if he gave an undertaking not to publish *The Gulag Archipelago* for twenty years.)

It was against this background that the decision was taken to punish Daniel and Sinyavsky, who had begun to publish manuscripts abroad in 1959, using the pseudonyms Nikolai Arzhak and Abram Tertz. It was not illegal to publish abroad; but it was illegal to publish anything, either at home or abroad, which was libellous or which defamed the Soviet state. It is an eloquent testimony to these writers' integrity and courage that they decided to publish their work pseudonymously for, in so doing, they deprived themselves of both fame and fortune. But they considered what they had to say to be of considerable importance.

Yuli Daniel was the son of a writer who had fought heroically in the revolutionary wars; he thus had both a good communist and a good literary background. He was severely wounded in the Second World War, and subsequently worked as a translator of poetry; he also wrote poetry which Akhmatova, among others, considered very good. Like his father, Yuli had a strong social conscience, and fearing that Stalinism was being revived, he began to write mildly satirical pieces lampooning it. In a story entitled 'Moscow Speaking', he describes what happens after it is announced officially over Moscow Radio that the Communist Party has authorized citizens to kill any other citizen except certain categories listed separately in an annexe to the decree. When the day of authorized killing arrives, the population shows itself to be remarkably peaceful and unvengeful – so much so that there is talk in official circles of 'sabotage'. The implication is that if the regime re-introduces terror as a weapon, the population will be too apathetic to resist. Mass terror, says the author, to be successful, requires the complicity of the victims. 'I feel that every member of society is responsible for what happens in it. I make no exception for myself.'

In another part of the same story he describes a group of friends in the garden of a *dacha* on a hot summer afternoon:

We must have been a strange sight – men and women of about thirty to thirty-five, stripped as if for the beach. We tactfully try to avoid the unexpected, comic and sad things about our appearance: the narrow shoulders, the incipient bald pates of the men, the hairy legs and thickened waists of the women. We had known each other for a long time in suits, dresses, coats and ties. But had not visualized ourselves in a state of nature practically without clothes. Who would have thought that Igor, so elegant and neat, and so successful with his women colleagues, would have bandy legs? Looking at each other in the raw was as interesting, amusing and shame making as looking at dirty postcards.

I found it hard to see anything very seditious in any of this. Neither could anyone else. The court, however, had no hesitation in finding that Daniel's writing lacked literary merit (which might have excused its content), was libellous and deserved the severest punishment. He was sentenced to five years of strict regime camp. Alexander Ginzburg (see page 54) wrote to Prime Minister Kosygin, to protest at both the trial and the sentence: 'I love my country and do not wish to see its name sullied by the latest unchecked activities of the KGB. I love Russian literature and do not want to see two more writers sent off under guard to fell trees.'

Daniel conducted himself with great courage during his captivity, refusing any privileges and refusing to recant. He described camp life in these terms:

The struggle against cold in the camp is waged in a unique way – they take away your clothes including sweaters. Solitary confinement [he had a number of spells of it for minor breaches of the regulations] is dog cold because you only get one blanket at night. The rest of the time you get bare boards or cement floors. [Bukovsky and many others confirm these awful facts.] Among the crimes punishable by solitary confinement is not waking up when they bang the bars, not standing up before an officer, brewing coffee or making toast, not going to political lectures, growing a few blades of dill in your area, or not fulfilling your work norm. The food is tasteless and lacking nourishment, it is impossible to buy fresh fruit or vegetables, the camp administration arbitrarily curtails or forbids visits by relatives, numerous parcels and letters are never received.

Daniel concludes that, although these conditions break the weak, they strengthen the resolve of the strong.*

Andrei Sinyavsky, using the pseudonym Abram Tertz, wrote in a gently mocking style like a refined Orwell. As was said at the time he was sentenced to seven years of hard regime camp, if he deserved such punishment then, on the same scale, Orwell deserved seventy years for *Animal Farm* alone. One novel to which the prosecution took great exception, *The Trial Begins*, was, like Daniel's work, a satire on the Stalin era and the kind of paranoia which leads people to conclude that 'everything in sight must be destroyed to make sure of the destruction of the enemy'. The narrator finds himself digging ditches in a concentration camp. Although he flushes his daily diary notes down the lavatory at home, they are recovered by the authorities who scrutinize everything their citizens produce, including the sewage. The notes soon find their way to the desk of the Chief Prosecutor, Globov, described as a model of the successful careerist. The KGB operators in the camp are described as 'kindly men of whom half the world is afraid'. One of them jeers at a prisoner, 'You reformers! I suppose you would like to see a kindly socialism; a free form of slavery?' Globov's son, Seryozha, an idealistic youth, dreams of a new world, communist and radiant, in which cleaning women would get the highest wages and government ministers the lowest. His grandmother reassures him, 'Of course there will be a world revolution. Now let me warm up something for you to eat.'

---

* The conditions of Soviet labour camps have not improved since Daniel's account. Indeed, they have worsened, as witnesses to the Fifth International Sakharov Hearing testified in April 1985. Geoffrey Seed has produced a film, *The Uranium Gulag*, compiled from some official Soviet documentary material and a good deal made secretly, which was screened on British TV on 17 July 1986. It graphically shows how appalling the conditions still are. Prison labour is being used at one uranium mine where protection against radiation hazards is almost nil. A former inmate, interviewed in this film, who had also been in a Nazi concentration camp, said that the differences were small – in the Soviet camps, prisoners were likely to die slowly. But overall the death rate of prisoners from malnutrition, over-work, and disease is very high.

Globov's wife Marina is beautiful but narcissistic; her morning exercises are described thus:

Marina stripped before the cheval glass and inspected her reflection. Its general outline reminded her of a propellor; taut blades running up and down from a narrow waist (she has had an abortion rather than see her beautiful waist expand). She made a business-like check-up – any sign of her buttocks sagging or wrinkles on her neck? (there weren't). Marina crouched on all fours with her tongue hanging out, an attitude which would embarrass most women. But not her, it only increased the sinuousness of her back and her elegance.

At an official dinner, Marina is sitting next to her lover, who is the Public Defender. He is thinking absent-mindedly about the possibility that human embryos, which go through a fish-like stage of development when they actually have gills, could be used (there being so many abortions) as a substitute for sardines to help overcome the food shortages. 'Vladimir,' Marina whispers, 'stop dreaming and eat your fish.'

If Sinyavsky could be a little tedious when he ventured into the philosophical, his purely ironical prose was amusing as this passage from *The Makepiece Experiment* illustrates. The hero, Leonard Makepiece, a bicycle mechanic in a small Russian town, is besotted with love for the elegant school teacher from Leningrad, Serafima. She considers Lenny too insignificant for her, as she makes clear:

'I like you very much, Serafima. Will you be my girl friend?'

'I see you do. But couldn't you be a bit more original?' she replies. She smoothes her hair with an indolent gesture, raising her elbow to show her breast to better advantage.

'I'll do anything for you,' Lenny avers, 'mend your wrist watch, arrange the doors of our future residence so they open at your approach. I'm a simple man but one day I shall be famous and then I will plaster your room with three-rouble notes so they look like green wallpaper.'

'You might at least make it 100-rouble notes,' says Serafima. 'Of course, money and riches are contemptible but I like a man to have ambition. You will have to start with having

the town here at your feet' – there was an intriguing smile on
her moist lips, an intoxicating promise in her eyes, and a
subtle hint in the tilt of her small, neat, appetizing nose.

'I don't know what I shall do,' says Lenny. 'But I shall do
my best.'

'The day you come to me borne on a shield and crowned
with vine leaves like Spartacus,' Serafima promises, 'we'll get
down to details.'

As the story continues, Lenny is able, temporarily, to gratify his
ambitions and Serafima's when, while renovating a room in an old
cottage, an ancient leather-bound book falls through the roof –
'fortunately not on my head', he later explains. It is a book of
ancient Hindu mysticism from which Lenny learns the art of
Charisma. This enables him to compel people to do his bidding.
Using this gift he produces a unique revolution (unique because it
is bloodless). He dispenses with the police and the army and
creates a truly Marxist paradise where the state has withered away
and the local river is flowing with champagne – so, at least, he is
able to induce the credulous population to believe.

Unfortunately Lenny's powers prove inadequate to deal with
the scepticism of the peasantry who, unlike the town dwellers, are
influenced purely by the bread supply. The agricultural problem
in the end defeats him (as it has done other Soviet leaders). The
cares of the state also intrude into his love life – he is much too
concerned by matters like reforming the currency and the spring
sowing to worry about Serafima – 'This puppet who expects me to
spend time and energy amusing her.' He advises her – like many
busy men before and since – 'Why don't you take up a hobby?
Culture, morals, the family, that sort of thing. Run along now –
I've got people waiting. I'll be in for dinner.' Ultimately, Lenny's
revolt is crushed with radio-controlled tanks that are impervious
to his Charisma.

An interesting aspect of the Daniel–Sinyavsky trial was that no
attempt was made by the prosecution to link the authors with such
obviously criminal activity as receiving money from foreign agencies, a tactic that was brought into play at later trials. Every effort
by the authors to explain that what they had written was literary
hyperbole and was not meant to be taken seriously, and so could

not be judged libellous, was either denied by the judge or howled down by the audience composed largely of hooligans picked up from the street for the purpose by the KGB.

A telegram protesting at the trial and its outcome was sent jointly by, amongst many others, Günter Grass, Graham Greene, François Mauriac, Arthur Miller and Ignazio Silone. Pavel Litvinov (Masha and Vera's cousin) provided foreign journalists with a detailed commentary on the 'evidence' of illegalities and the court procedures. He was one of the first Soviet dissidents to take the risk of involving foreign journalists in the human rights question.*

Litvinov realized that if the resurgence of Stalinism was to be aborted, it would be necessary to alert public opinion in the West. In a very effective letter to the London *Times* (13 January 1968) he described how the trials of dissidents were being held in circumstances which made a mockery of the idea of impartial justice – the courts were packed with officials from the KGB and members of the militia who mocked the witnesses as well as the accused and created the atmosphere of a lynching. This letter created a furore in the West. A telegram supporting Pavel included the following signatories: Cecil Day Lewis, W. H. Auden and Stephen Spender (both once overt supporters of the Soviet Union), Henry Moore, A. J. Ayer, Bertrand Russell, Julian Huxley, Mary McCarthy, J. B. Priestley, Jacquetta Hawkes, Paul Scofield, Igor Stravinsky, Stuart Hampshire, Maurice Bowra and Mrs George Orwell. In a letter to Stephen Spender thanking him for this support Pavel explained that the telegram was never received but that the text of it had been heard from a BBC broadcast. Nevertheless it had had an effect on the authorities.†

The proceedings of the Daniel–Sinyavsky case were fully documented in a *White Book* compiled by Alexander Ginzburg. He was arrested in January 1967 together with three associates, Yuri

---

* Such action exposed those who took it to the serious additional charge of working for foreign agencies. It was on such a false charge that Shcharansky was sentenced to thirteen years in a prison camp.

† Largely arising from this correspondence, a trust was established to enable a journal, *Index on Censorship*, to be founded. This was devoted to publishing censored authors from all over the world and to defending the precious right of free speech no matter where it might be threatened. Its first editor was Michael Scammell.

Galanskov, Alexei Dobrovolsky and Vera Lashkova; with the exception of Lashkova, who was a typist, they were all prominent dissidents who had had previous altercations with the authorities. All were charged with anti-Soviet agitation and propaganda and Galanskov with dealing in foreign currency. Dobrovolsky, it was claimed, had links with the NTS (see page 60) – which was probably the only truthful allegation made. This trial is believed to have aroused such a widespread reaction among the Russian intelligentsia that it was the main impetus to the establishment of the *Chronicle of Current Events*, a brave and dangerous, and ultimately futile, attempt to protect the innocent victims of state terror by telling the truth about it.

Pavel Litvinov documented the trial in a book of 200,000 words entitled *The Trial of the Four*. It was a scholarly exposition; Bertrand Russell wrote of it: 'So intolerably unjust were the procedures of the court, that even the official journal of the British Communist Party, normally a faithful spokesman of the Soviet Union, felt compelled to publish criticism of it.' Although the trial was nominally an open one, very few members of the public or even relatives of the accused were admitted. But as many as a hundred protestors gathered outside the court house and it was proceedings such as this which converted Andrei Sakharov from being a socially conscious scientist into a human rights activist. He met his wife, Elena Bonner, at such a gathering.

Galanskov got seven years in a strict regime camp, Ginzburg five years, Dobrovolsky two years and Lashkova one year.

Besides the protests outside the court, many letters and petitions were written in protest at these trials. The signatories were mostly punished in the various ways available – dismissal from the Communist Party, demotion or dismissal from senior jobs and from universities and academic institutes being the commonest.

The protest movement was not by any means daunted by this evidence of official displeasure. The next major event to provoke it into action – and the authorities into counter-action – was the invasion of Czechoslovakia on 20 August 1968. The process of liberalization which the Czech government under Dubček had set in motion was viewed by the intelligentsia of the Soviet Union with fascination, and by the authorities with undisguised abhorrence. The Dubček regime was crushed with an efficient ruthlessness which left the whole world feeling angry and bruised. A few days later, a small group of protestors which included Natalya Gorbanevskaya, Viktor Fainberg and Pavel Litvinov gathered in Pushkin Square and unfurled banners proclaiming 'Hands off Czechoslovakia' and 'For Your Freedom and Ours'. However, the KGB were waiting and the banners were seized almost immediately and the protestors (except Natalya who had her three-month-old son with her) were bundled into waiting cars and taken away.

The demonstrators were subsequently brought to trial in an atmosphere of official hostility that was brutally frank. The court was packed and many of the spectators (chosen by the KGB) were drunk and hurled abuse and threats at the defendants. Pavel Litvinov was exiled for five years (he was allowed to go abroad in 1974 and now lives in the United States). Natalya was referred to a psychiatric clinic and declared 'not-responsible'.

The blatant disregard by the authorities for the legal rights of the citizenry under the Soviet constitution coupled with the ever-widening net of repression which encompassed religious believers, would-be emigrants, writers, 'reformists', in short, anyone with awkward views, provoked the formation of a Human Rights Committee in Moscow of which Andrei Sakharov and Valery Chalidze were the prime movers. The purpose of the Committee was simply to provide help to people caught up in the repression, to give legal advice and comfort, and to agitate for the observance of the law. This plea for legality lay at the heart of most human rights agitation at that time. Of course the reality of the Soviet legal system is the all-pervading unwritten law which overrides all other laws – no action which the authorities consider 'threatens socialism' is legal, and they are the sole arbiters of what constitutes such a threat.

CHAPTER 8

VICTORY FOR BUKOVSKY

In December 1976 David Markham rang me with the news that Vladimir Bukovsky was to be released. Apparently an exchange with Luis Corvalan, the Chilean communist leader, had been arranged. Although at this stage it was only a rumour, David had arranged to fly to Geneva to meet Bukovsky who was said to be already on his way there. Actually he arrived next day to be greeted with the sort of reception normally afforded to pop stars, and rarely even to them.

Bukovsky had become a hero overnight. Most people had never heard his name, but this soon changed, for his story struck a very responsive chord. First there was his incredible courage, his refusal to allow the harshest treatment to break his spirit; then there was the realization that the ideas for which this young man had sacrificed thirteen years of his life were basic to the question of human dignity; finally there was a sigh of relief at this indication that the Soviet Bear, previously so immovable, so heedless of public opinion, could in fact be made to shift its ground. This victory gave the world hope of a brighter future. I noted in my diary that Bukovsky would come to be classed with Wilberforce and Martin Luther King as amongst mankind's most important defenders. He had certainly achieved more for freedom, I thought, than the thousands of hoodlums with their Kalashnikov rifles who terrorize the world in the name of liberty.

Bukovsky was apparently kept in handcuffs until his plane had flown out of Soviet airspace. What they expected a half-starved and unarmed man to attempt is difficult to imagine. Perhaps they feared he might demand to be returned to Moscow! His first statement on arrival in Geneva was that he hoped the many other prisoners in Russia, more deserving than himself, would not be forgotten. When asked how many political prisoners there were in the Soviet Union, he replied: 'Two hundred and fifty million.'

I commented in my diary that David Markham, unassuming

and gentle, but resolute when his sense of justice was aroused, represents the sort of man, easy to underestimate, who makes the British people formidable when attacked. He is also a witness (Rosemary Winckley is another) to the fact that ordinary people still count.

The release of Bukovsky was the first tacit admission by the Soviet government that it held people in prison for their views. They have always denied this strenuously, claiming that political prisoners are only found in fascist states. One question often put to Bukovsky was: how did prisoners, faced with the possibility of indefinite confinement in harsh conditions, perpetually cold and hungry, deprived of all comforts, needs, security, and love, maintain their sanity let alone their defiance? His answer was that many prisoners could sustain neither, but that others, fortified by 'inner freedom', did succeed. There can be no doubt that, in releasing Bukovsky, a witness to the brutality of their system whose testimony had great credibility, the Soviet Union suffered a humiliating defeat. Why did they do it? No one really knew but the principal reason appeared to be pressure from Western communist parties, particularly those of France and Italy, which were trying to rid themselves of the image of brutality, illegality and tyranny which the very word communism inspired in many people.

But, almost as if it hoped to demonstrate to the world that the release of Bukovsky did not mean that a free rein was to be given to dissenters in the Soviet Union, the KGB re-arrested Vladimir Borisov, a well-known figure in the human rights movement.* As soon as news of Borisov's arrest was received, David Markham arranged a protest vigil outside the Soviet embassy. At his instigation, Professor Henry Dicks, a past President of the Royal College of Psychiatrists, sent a telegram to the doctor in charge of

---

* Borisov was born in Leningrad, the son of an engineer. At the age of eighteen, he organized a dock strike, probably the first ever in the Soviet Union. Masha, who greatly admired him (as did many other dissidents I met later), told me that his resilience and humour were such that he could disarm the toughest KGB persecutor. He had been a victim of psychiatric terror, having been kept for nine out of the previous thirteen years in psychiatric hospitals and forcibly injected with mind-affecting drugs. It was he who collected much of the documentary evidence of psychiatric abuse which Bukovsky used in compiling the *Manual of Psychiatry for Dissenters*.

the Leningrad psychiatric hospital where Borisov was being detained. It said:

> British psychiatrists learn with horror of the shameful re-arrest and mistreatment of Vladimir Borisov in your hospital. Unless this ceases, your name and that of your associates will be linked in history with the Nazis whose methods you have copied. Shame on you and your contemptible masters.

I did not imagine the hospital director would exactly enjoy receiving this telegram which reflected the indignation of many doctors (and others) at what was clearly intended to be a face-saving *quid pro quo* for the Bukovsky furore.

Borisov was refused permission to receive a visit from his wife. When he tried to speak to her through the bars of the psychiatric prison window, he was subjected to the barbarous 'dry wrapper'. This involves wrapping the subject tightly in bed sheets (sometimes moistened canvas is used). The body heat which is generated, and the shrinkage of the binding, is intensely painful and can cause death. Borisov's wife rang to tell us of the arrest and to say that he had been offered his release if he would agree to go into exile abroad. He refused this offer, saying he would only consider it if he was first declared sane.*

On Christmas Day 1976, eight days after Bukovsky's release, we had a special Christmas dinner for our own family and the Litvinov granddaughters and their children. It was a happy occasion – I think the first time they had ever attended a traditional English Xmas with roast turkey, plum pudding flaming in brandy sauce, and, of course, funny hats and crackers with ridiculous, incomprehensible jokes. They must have felt a long way from their homeland and no doubt they felt nostalgic and sad, especially for their friends suffering in prison camps and in exile.

* * *

* I met the Borisovs later in Russia. They are an impressive couple. Dr Sidney Bloch, a prominent English psychiatrist, had examined him while visiting Leningrad and found him sane. So did a Soviet commission. Borisov was released on 5 March 1977.

Vladimir Bukovsky arrived in London on 4 January 1977. I noted that he received the sort of welcome that Mick Jagger might have envied. It was ironical that the day before the news of his release was received, David Markham and I had discussed the possibility of getting some warm clothing for him. Now he was a superstar, so much in demand for interviews and lecture tours that he would soon need a manager to handle his affairs and the resultant fees.*

On 13 January, David Markham came to see me. He was obviously exhausted and deflated; it had been planned that Bukovsky would spend two weeks with him in seclusion at his little country cottage, but this proved impossible. The place had rapidly been besieged by journalists and cameramen and the telephone never stopped ringing. Every organization in the world with any interest in human rights, and a number with rather dubious motives, were clamouring for access to him. David seemed bitter that the media, who had, by and large, ignored his pleas for publicity during the six-year campaign for Bukovsky, were now posing as stalwart defenders of freedom. More disturbing, however, was the fact that Bukovsky had been taken under the wing of people whose devotion to right-wing causes appeared to be greatly in excess of their concern with human rights.

Among the people most insistent on attaching themselves to Bukovsky, were some members of a somewhat dubious anti-Soviet group, mainly descendants of White Russian emigrés. Others had links with a shadowy organization which goes by the initials, NTS.†

The arrival of Bukovsky in the UK provoked widespread discus-

---

* I think this happened. On the day I made this entry, I recorded the view that the widespread publicity about the abuse of psychiatry which the Bukovsky case had aroused would likely lead to the Serbsky Institute going the way of the camps at Belsen and Auschwitz. But so far, it hasn't.

† Members of this organization seem to crop up wherever Soviet emigrés are in evidence. With headquarters in Frankfurt, it had an ambiguous record of collaboration with Hitlerism in its early days; but being composed largely of intensely patriotic Russians, it fell out with Nazism after the German invasion of Russia, when many of its leaders were interned. The NTS has a strong religious (Orthodox) basis and it stands politically for a democratic, if still socialist Russia. It has pervasive internal links in the Soviet Union which enabled it to receive information rather freely. This makes it particularly suspect to the KGB. Possession of NTS literature or suspicion of links with the organization is a certain prescription for a sojourn in a hard regime prison camp.

sion in the media and among people generally about the human rights problem in the USSR. Some people, echoing the Soviet line, questioned the right of outsiders to be involved in the internal affairs of another country. The Soviet government claimed that the US administration had no right to give encouragement to Soviet dissidents, becoming still more vociferous when President Carter announced after his election that human rights would be the central concern of his administration. What then, I wondered, was the point of the United Nations Covenant on Civil and Political Rights, to which the Soviet Union is a signatory?

The Covenant is legally binding on its signatories and quite clearly makes it the business of the international community to concern itself with any behaviour which is inconsistent with the norms of civilization, because therein lies the greatest danger to peace. While protesting that support for its dissidents is an intolerable interference in its internal affairs, the Soviets have never forsaken the right to render help to whoever may be causing a ruckus in countries outside its own orbit. Any group of trouble-makers, no matter how lacking in popular support they may be, can rely on Soviet help if it tags the word 'liberation' to its title. Communist parties in the West, sworn to the revolutionary overthrow of their government, can rely on Soviet backing (provided they are not supporters of Peking). But apparently this is not an interference in anybody's internal affairs. This attitude is farcical, and tragic. (Sakharov has warned that both superpowers are guilty of undue meddling in areas of conflict outside their true spheres and that this constitutes a great threat to peace.) Of course the Soviet Union is not the only country with a bad record of human rights violation, but it is certainly the only one with the power to change the course of human destiny. It is obviously not in the same category as a banana republic with a tin-pot tyrant running the show. I do not condone breaches of human rights wherever they occur and I was glad to see at the time that Daniel Patrick Moynihan, one of America's most forceful and interesting political personalities, was taking a very strong stand against the Carter administration's support for a World Bank loan of 60 million dollars for Chile. This double standard (American support for the Shah of Iran was another example) sullies America's reputation as the defender of human rights. It will rebound on them eventually, and on us, if we stand idly by and refuse to condemn it.

CHAPTER 9

ANDREI AMALRIK, SOVIET GAD-FLY

At the end of 1976 a number of interesting former Soviet citizens gathered in London on the occasion of an exhibition of Unofficial Art from the Soviet Union. One of the most stimulating of them was Andrei Amalrik the historian, whose book, *Can the Soviet Union Survive till 1984?* had created a considerable stir, not least among the top officials of the KGB. (His final answer is yes, but that in the process it will suffer considerable instability which will constitute a threat to the stability of the world system.)

My first meeting with Amalrik was at a party arranged by a group of Russian emigrés who seemed to be inclined to counter-revolutionary politics of a rather unrealistic (and frightening) character. Many seemed to be the descendants of the old Russian aristocracy. Possibly they had links with the NTS (see page 60*n*) but I had no real knowledge of this. I do know I got a sound ticking off when I spoke of the 'Russian government' during some political discussion. I was told in no uncertain terms that there was no 'Russian government'. There was a 'Soviet government' which was illegal, temporary and totally lacking in legitimacy. It did not speak in the name of the Russian people but only in its own name and its crimes were not to be laid at the feet of the helpless Russian people who, one day, would rise up and regain their destiny.

Amalrik was a somewhat controversial figure – regarded by some emigrés as light weight, more interested in self-promotion than in counter-revolution, and in personal notoriety than in true reform. Be that as it may, I found him stimulating, original, humorous and serious, also convincing; a man of strong beliefs, considerable knowledge and integrity. I had a number of talks with him during the following week. He was then about thirty-nine years old and had been against the Soviet system since childhood. It was not just an intellectual opposition but something deeper. As he expressed it, 'I am against the system not because it is dishonest, but from organic revulsion. I can't listen to Soviet radio or read the Soviet press, all the media are dishonest and full of lies.' (I concluded that Amalrik would not find much difference in the Western media, which, in the end, he did not.) He was obsessively honest to the point of intolerance; the sort of person who would have found it difficult to accept official dictation anywhere, and certainly incapable of adapting to the deceptions which all governments practise. Amalrik was clearly an outsider, a born outcast, a character from a Camus novel. I thought him the most likeable of all the male Soviet dissidents I had met up to this point.

It was obvious that someone so gifted and courageous could have gone far in the Soviet system if he had wanted to toe the party line and had been willing to help his career along by informing on his friends and assisting the propaganda organs. But he was one of the few who subscribed to Solzhenitsyn's maxim: 'Better dead than a scoundrel'. Amalrik was the son of an archaeologist and trained as a historian; but his training had remained incomplete, as he ruefully admitted, because of the frequency of his conflicts with authority. He never completed his university degree and none of the five plays he had written have ever been produced in the USSR. In 1963 he was expelled from Moscow University for submitting an essay which claimed that the early Russian state centred on Kiev in the tenth century owed much of its civilization to the Normans. He had taken the paper to the Danish embassy to be forwarded to a Danish scholar who apparently held similar views. The KGB soon made it clear that such heresy was a crime that would not be taken lightly in the Soviet Union. In 1965 he was sent to a camp in Siberia for 'parasitism'. He began to write his notorious book after his release, explaining in the introduction that a certain absence of scholarly detail was due to lack of access to appropriate facilities! He asked his Western readers to take the same view as an ichthyologist would take if he found one of his fish talking; he hoped that personal experience would be accepted as a substitute for academic research!

Amalrik concluded that there were three main and distinct opposition points of view in the Soviet Union, none of which represented a real threat to the system, or even envisaged a fundamental alteration. The first advocated a return to strict

Marxist-Leninist orthodoxy, the second, a restoration of Christian morality and the third the adoption of a modified Western-style 'social democracy' with the state still playing the major role in ownership of the means of production but with greater freedom for the individual and a more pluralistic society.

I found that his description of Soviet society more or less tallied with what I had heard from other dissidents. He was highly critical of the so-called élite, the privileged bureaucracy, especially because he thought that the continuous weeding out of people with original ideas, initiative and independence of mind through forced emigration, exile, psychiatric internment and other forms of intimidation had reduced its membership to a level of mediocrity which would, in the end, lead to a catastrophe.

The attitude of the ordinary bureaucrat, according to Amalrik, was that he was such an insignificant cog in such a vast piece of machinery that any thought of doing anything except what he has been told to do would be ludicrous and also potentially dangerous. So long as he did nothing to upset the system, he had done his duty; he was not expected to do more and any effort to do more might well rebound to his disadvantage. Thus inertia and complacency were inbuilt (many Americans would say that the same attitudes are common at General Motors). Amalrik considered that power in the Soviet Union was no longer directed towards furthering a coherent purpose or ideology – its function was primarily to preserve itself. And those with the most power were most active in the preservation of it – self-preservation had become the dominant motive of action. Reform, innovation, development, no matter how obviously desirable or how urgent, came up against this obstacle. The system had seized up partly because of its very nature and partly because of the special character of the Russian people.

The Russians have no tradition of personal freedom, self-government, and equality before the law, nor of the personal responsibility without which a society based upon these principles cannot succeed. To the average Russian, the idea of freedom suggests not the opportunity of securing a good life for himself, but the danger that some clever fellow will make good at his expense. To many people, the idea of 'freedom' is synonymous with the opportunity to indulge in some kind of anti-social activity with impunity. And so far as the rights of the individual are concerned, the idea that the human personality could represent some kind of value is preposterous – only strength and authority can be respected.

Clearly the humanist revolution which has so changed the nature of Western European society has passed the Russians by. The question is – will they ever catch up? Years of indoctrination have taught the Soviet people that individual desires must be subjected to the needs of the collective. Anything else is immoral, dangerous and wrong. A depressing number of Soviet emigrés to the West still believe this and find the 'freedom' which they longed for while in the USSR a disappointing illusion. One of the ironies of Soviet emigration policy is that if the Soviet people were allowed to come and go freely, as indeed they should be according to international law, it might prove that as many would come back as left the country.

The idea of collective rather than individual freedom has taken deep root in the Soviet psyche because, according to Amalrik, the Russians tend to be particularly prone to envy. It is very important to them that no one should be better off than they are. In the West, the idea that someone is doing better may provoke envy, but so long as people have at least a chance to better themselves, the envy is bearable and rarely decisive in forming attitudes. But Russians find someone else's success more painful than their own failure. Amalrik explained this depressing scenario as deriving from the peasant background which still dominates Soviet life. Only affluence and middle-class attitudes will bring real change.

But change is bound to come and perhaps faster than expected, particularly as more and more Russians are permitted to travel abroad. In fact, the desire for foreign travel is becoming almost irresistible. Holidays on the Black Sea are not enough. The *babushkas* want Ibiza.*

Amalrik said the current situation in the Soviet Union resembled that which preceded the revolutions in 1905 and 1917. Society

* Mrs Gorbachev's chic, which is so widely displayed, was intended to impress the West with the extent of modernization in the Soviet Union – an attempt to dispel the 'steel-capped teeth' image. But it has backfired. There are now a lot of well-to-do Russians who have made their money in dealings in the 'second market' and would like to dress as smartly as Mrs Gorbachev. As their numbers increase, and their patience decreases, there will be some interesting developments.

then was caste-ridden and immobile, and the government paralyzed (this was certainly true of the last days of the Brezhnev regime) and unable to make the needed reforms. The nationalities question was becoming ever more pressing (just as it is today) and the bureaucracy began to pursue an ever more adventurous foreign policy to divert attention from the problems at home. The Russo-Japanese war and the First World War were the results of these policies to a larger extent than is realized.

Amalrik's views on the Soviet relations with China were equally interesting, if a bit far-fetched. He saw that a conflict with China was inevitable because Russia was the only country with land which was not already over-populated, and which was within China's grasp because of its massive population resources. Obviously China could not expand to the south or across the Pacific Ocean to attack America. Amalrik was particularly scathing about American policy, accusing America of encouraging communism in countries which do not want it or cannot benefit from it – Eastern Europe for example – while opposing it in countries who largely want and need communism – such as Viet-Nam.

Amalrik's origins were interesting. He said he stemmed from the Visigoths; that there were two kings of Jerusalem in the twelfth century named Amalrik, and that one of his ancestors was a papal legate who, when asked how, on the capture of a town in the Albigensian crusade, God would distinguish the Catholics from the infidels, replied: 'Kill them all, God will know his own.'

Amalrik derided the idea that exposing the Russians to the superficial aspects of American culture – Coca-cola, mini-skirts, pop music – would, in the end, humanize Soviet society. He said that there will never be a socialism with a human face, only one with bare knees.

The most depressing aspect of Amalrik's vision of Soviet society was his view that the dominant position of the Russian peasantry had created an intellectual milieu that was characterized by insecurity, stubbornness and inflexibility and which was basically brutal and aggressive. There is an underlying fear of insignificance and incompetence which is not understood by non-Russians and which makes negotiation difficult, even impossible. The Russians dare not appear weak, and are fearful that concessions will be regarded as weakness. He regarded the growing nationalities problem as the greatest source of Soviet weakness and argued that it would ultimately lead to the dissolution of the Soviet Empire (just like all other empires) or else to a war of desperation.

Amalrik believed, as did Bukovsky and Solzhenitsyn, that Russia was actively preparing for war – that the intensity of its military preparations had reached an unstoppable momentum.

One of Amalrik's most engaging characteristics was his sense of humour which I found unusual for a Russian dissident – most of them tend to have grim 'gallows' humour, or, more often, no sense of humour at all. He recounted his experiences in a Siberian prison camp for hours as if he was describing a seaside holiday. In his prison there was apparently quite a bevy of wife murderers. One of these men approached Amalrik (having taken some months to decide that he was not a KGB stool pigeon) to ask him to write a letter on his behalf to the authorities protesting the severity of his fifteen year prison sentence. Apparently the judge had accepted that there had been fifteen blows with an axe when, in fact, there had only been seven. Inevitably, the appeal was rejected; but the murderer consoled himself by explaining that it might have been worse, in fact he had used twenty blows!

After Amalrik's release he was given the option of recanting his views or emigrating to Israel. As he was not Jewish, and as his wife was a Moslem, the suggestion of emigrating to Israel seemed a curious one. But apparently it was simply to allow authority to claim it (emigration) to be part of 'family unification' and in no way an indication of dissatisfaction with the reality of Soviet life.

On 24 February 1980 Amalrik demonstrated outside the Elysée Palace after President Valéry Giscard d'Estaing refused him an audience. He had been very forthright in describing Marchais as an unrepentant Stalinist despite the obvious attempts by the French (and Italian) Communist Parties to distance themselves from the worst features of the Soviet system with its remnants of Stalinist oppression and intolerance. The French Party had even denounced the concept of the 'dictatorship of the proletariat' claiming it to be nothing but a Stalinist device to enslave the working class and place a new bureaucratic class above them. Meanwhile Amalrik had been severely criticized for his demonstration against d'Estaing (showing off again) but he strongly defended himself in the same terms as Bukovsky – 'outside voices' were, he said, the only weapons the dissident movement in the

USSR had, and every opportunity to support them must be taken. There should be no economic or political concessions from the West to the USSR unless and until they showed they were prepared to observe their commitments under international law (and the Helsinki Final Act) to human rights.*

Amalrik was insistent that the West should show no weakness or division on this issue. It certainly must not accept the Soviet line that human rights were a purely internal Soviet concern and that any attempt to influence them on this question was an interference with their sovereignty.

Tragically, Amalrik died in a motor car accident in Spain in April 1980 (see Chapter 17). There was a widely held belief that the KGB had engineered this, but no real evidence to support the claim (although certainly it is a possibility).

---

* It is interesting how many important dissidents take this view, for example Shcharansky and Sakharov.

CHAPTER 10

SOCREALISM:
Notes from my Diary

19 January 1977

Last night we went with Masha and Vera to an exhibition of 'Unofficial' art from the Soviet Union at the Institute of Contemporary Art in the Mall. The work in the exhibition came largely from the collection of Alexander (Sasha) Glezer, who is a poet and earned his living in the USSR as a translator, especially of Georgian poetry in which field he claimed to have been a world authority having published fifteen books of translations. (I think he is prone to exaggeration but who isn't?) He is certainly an ardent collector but how he obtained his paintings is a bit of a mystery. Of course, many of the works would have been given him, others he probably bought cheaply as it is virtually illegal for unofficial artists (i.e. non-members of the Artists' Union) to sell their works. Apparently the authorities turn a blind eye to sales to foreigners and this is a growing market, especially with Americans. Sasha now lives in Paris (he emigrated in February 1975) where he has established a permanent exhibition of Soviet unofficial art using his collection as a nucleus. It is certainly comprehensive; there were 96 paintings on display at the ICA. The immediate effect is disappointing – the work seems so derivative. Surrealism is the dominant influence but German expressionism is not far behind. Primitivism is in evidence, so are copies of outmoded American styles – op art, pop art and such like. When one considers that before the revolution, Russian artists like Kandinsky, Malevich, Tatlin and Lissitsky, to name only the most obvious, were leading the way into the twentieth century, it is daunting to see this evidence of the stifling hand of totalitarianism on creativity.

Many of the artists whose work was on display were present at the opening, having been forced into exile. They included Ernst Neizvestny, by any standards a remarkable man and a great sculptor. I wondered how the Soviet Union could afford to banish such human beings from their society. Either they have inexhaustible human resources or, as is more likely, they don't know what they are doing. I talked to Diana Gould (Yehudi Menuhin's wife) who told me that when she met Shostakovich in Moscow his hands shook so much, due to fear induced by his rows with Stalin, that he couldn't do up his buttons.

All art in the Soviet Union is controlled by the state. Not only is it the provider of the funds, it is also the arbiter of style and content. The intervention of Stalin into the realm of poetry has been described. But his intervention in artistic matters was all-embracing. He even compelled Prokofiev and Shostakovich to modify music to which he objected on ideological grounds. In the early days of the revolution, art in all its many forms was allowed to flourish without hindrance. There was, in consequence, an unrivalled outburst of creativity in every field of art but especially painting. Chagall said of this period, 'Lenin turned the world upside down, just as I do in my paintings.' But by the early thirties, a clamp had been applied; art was compelled to conform to the tenets of Socialist Realism. In effect, art was to be an extension of the propaganda machinery of the state. Above all, it was to be comprehensible to the masses; it had to glorify their achievements and elevate their (drooping) spirits. Naturally, this official straitjacket had the reverse effect. Andrei Sinyavsky derisively described 'socrealism' as an art form which makes 'whores as modest as maidens and hangmen as tender as mothers'.

From Sasha, I learned that painting which did not conform to the officially approved style was not in itself illegal, provided it remained a private activity and the paintings were neither exhibited nor sold. A great stimulus to unofficial art derived from the Sixth World Festival of Youth which was held in Moscow in the summer of 1957. Intended as a goodwill propaganda exercise, it included a large exhibition of paintings by young painters from the 52 participating countries. This was the first opportunity Russian artists had had to see a wide selection of works from the outside world. The impact was powerful and the effect very different to that intended by the organizers. The newly liberated Russian painters were soon in trouble – their works derided as 'permeated by the corrupting influence of reactionary bourgeois ideology'. Talented pupils were excluded from painting schools, and gifted artists, deprived of their official standing in the Artists' Union (for their decadent art), had to work as doorkeepers, night watchmen, and hospital attendants. The growing number of unofficial artists led, inevitably, to increasing efforts to circumvent the official ban on exhibiting their work. At first, such exhibitions were held privately, some in social clubs and in scientific institutes. Neizvestny even succeeded in having a show at Moscow University. Things came to a head in December 1962 when Khrushchev visited an exhibition staged by the Moscow Section of the Artists' Union (MOSK). A number of works by 'formalists' (i.e. painters who deviated from the norms of socrealism and painted in their own style) had been deliberately infiltrated into the show by the leaders of the art establishment. Khrushchev reacted violently (and predictably), abusing the offending artists for their corrupt bourgeois tastes and declaring that much better art could be achieved by the random swishing of a donkey's tail daubed with paint. This was the signal for a severe crackdown on *avant-garde* artists. This, of course, inhibited, but did not stop, them. Sasha Glezer organized an unofficial exhibition in January 1967 in the rooms of a workers' club, the manager being a friend. But it attracted so much publicity from Western journalists that it was soon ordered to be closed. Sasha describes the subsequent interview with a KGB officer ensconced in the club manager's chair:

'This exhibition is a put-up job by the CIA,' said the KGB man.
'I put it up myself,' Sasha replied.
'Then you are a blind tool of the CIA,' was the response.

Sasha later organized an exhibition from his own collection in Tbilisi. The inhabitants, he claims, were flabbergasted saying, 'We never thought such a thing could happen here. We actually have some real art.'

As the repression of unofficial artists increased, so did their determination to exhibit their work to the Russian public at large. A group of them decided to hold an outdoor exhibition which was arranged for September 1974. They notified the Moscow City Council of their plans in a letter. As there were no regulations which forbad open air exhibitions, officialdom was temporarily nonplussed. (The organizers had carefully chosen a piece of waste land for their site so that they could not be charged with causing

71

an obstruction, or worse still, 'disturbing public order'.) The authorities decided to meet this challenge ruthlessly, heedless of the consequences (in the event, the adverse publicity was enormous and very damaging). The artists were bundled into lorries (which happened to be passing) by plain-clothed citizens (who happened to be present and very angry). When this manoeuvre by the KGB proved insufficient, a bulldozer appeared and flattened the remaining canvases and nearly flattened Oscar Rabin (a famous painter). It was all over in forty minutes. Two of the arrested painters were later served with military call-up papers and three were confined in a psychiatric hospital. Many Western journalists and photographers were present and several had teeth knocked out besides being drenched by the water cannon which was called in.

Since these events, the official attitude to artists has not changed, 'socrealism' is still the only tolerated art form, and in consequence more and more artists are leaving or trying to leave the Soviet Union. However, according to Sasha, most artists, no matter how deep their conflict with authority, resist the temptation to accept exile because of the fear that their artistic impulse will be diminished once the roots of it, their contact with their home land, are severed.*

26 January

Last night we went to the ICA with Sasha to see a film made by a BBC team on Ernst Neizvestny, who was in the audience. It has a magnificent commentary spoken by John Berger whose rich voice makes him sound like Richard Burton. Neizvestny, thickset, vital and good-humoured, reminded me of Zorba the Greek. So, all in all, it was an entertaining evening. Neizvestny explained to us that after being wounded in battle, and being given up for dead, he had discarded a lot of inessential psychological baggage and this had helped him greatly in the continuous fight with authority which has characterized his life as an artist. Although expelled

---

* Recently, Gorbachev has said that more freedom of expression is to be allowed, but it is too soon to say if this has happened. It is ironical that much of the art which is officially rejected in the Soviet Union, whether poetry, prose or painting, would bring honour to it, if its display was freely permitted.

from membership of the Artists' Union, and therefore unable to continue to compete for commissions for official projects (at which he had previously been very successful) he still managed to survive as an unofficial artist and even to be commissioned to make a few sculptures, including one to commemorate the completion of the Aswan Dam. Despite having many verbal altercations with Khrushchev, Neizvestny said that he admired him for his courageous exposure of Stalin's crimes. Officially, Khrushchev strongly disapproved of Neizvestny's work. He once described it as 'a nauseating concoction which fills us with indignation that a man, obviously not lacking promise, and having completed his education in a state institution, repays the people with such black ingratitude.' But after Khrushchev's death, his son asked Neizvestny to make a head stone for his father's grave. Apparently this was Khrushchev's wish. Despite this honour, or perhaps because of it, the KGB raided Neizvestny's studio and smashed everything breakable including the plaster casts of his work in progress. He was confronted with the choice of prison or exile. He now lives in New York.

I came away from this meeting wondering where men like this get their courage. He could easily have had a brilliant life (like the poet Yevtushenko): rich by any standards, with a nice apartment, a *dacha* in a sunny spot in the country, a flash car, and above all, the freedom to travel abroad. All that would have been required was that he toe the party line – more or less. But this price he would not pay.*

Later, Neizvestny spoke very amusingly about his experiences at university after the war:

We learnt about what Lenin said from what Stalin said about Lenin. We learnt about what Marx had said from what Lenin

---

* Yevtushenko is something of an enigma. Undoubtedly he is a fine poet, and often outspokenly critical of the regime; nevertheless, every Russian I have spoken to distrusts him. They say that the frequency with which he is allowed to travel abroad is sufficient to brand him as someone highly trusted by the KGB. It is one of the latter's ploys to allow people who are liked and trusted abroad to express criticism with impunity. Such people can be very useful for spreading disinformation and for other purposes. I do not personally subscribe to such a miserable scenario involving a fine poet, but many people with infinitely greater experience of the inner working of the Soviet system than I, do. They ask: 'If he is an honest man, why isn't he in jail?'

had said about Marx. We learnt about what Hegel said from what Marx said about Hegel. In the end, we taught ourselves realizing that what we were being taught was nonsense.

His description of the intellectual isolation of Soviet artists was daunting. For example, John Berger had written that he, Neizvestny, was greatly influenced by Brancusi, when in fact, or so he told us, he knew nothing of Brancusi or for that matter of most Western artists. Of the country which he greatly loved, Russia, he said that there was no vestige there of communism nor even of socialism. 'Socialism exists only in the imagination of man,' he said. 'The reality is hideous.'

Neizvestny's strongly anti-Soviet views were echoed soon after his arrival in Zurich (to which he first emigrated) by the publication in Lausanne of a satirical book based, in part, on his life, entitled *Yawning Heights*. The author was his friend, Alexander Zinoviev, a mathematical logician as well as a satirist.*

The book is set in a country called Ibansk in which a new social order called 'socism' is being built. The building of a new society is acknowledged to be difficult and phasic. In the first phase of Ibansk's existence, called USELESS EXISTENCE, one third of the population are in camps and another third are guarding them. In the second phase, CONFUSION, which follows the death of THE GREAT MASTER, who presided over phase one, a new leadership under a MANAGER is set up. The intention is to create phase three, PROSPERITY, but this is still a long way off. Those who prosper in Ibansk are the licensed intellectuals who serve the state faithfully and propagate its message. It is they who get the keys to the theatre boxes controlled by the Security Service (someone resembling Yevtushenko has a key). Those who care about real knowl-

---

* Alexander Zinoviev is one of the Soviet Union's most important critics. He was a pilot in the Second World War but his strongly and openly expressed anti-Stalinist views led to his exile in 1978. He now lives in Munich. He popularized the use of the term *Homo sovieticus* to describe the sort of creature that seventy years of exposure to communist indoctrination had turned his beloved Russians into. It is clear that besides hatred there is some love and even admiration for the product – 'a creature infinitely flexible, resourceful and ever ready to shift his moral position to suit his circumstances'. The virus responsible for these characteristics, Zinoviev claims, is becoming world-wide. He is one of many emigrés who is appalled by the complacency with which the West accepts the invasion.

edge (they have names like Schizophrenic, Babbler, Gossip and Slanderer) are either committing suicide, going to jail, dying or emigrating. The cleverest, Schizophrenic, says: 'I am criticizing no one. I am suggesting nothing. I am just thinking.' At the crematorium where intractable cases are sent, there is a notice above the entrance – 'Take the urn with your ashes with you as you leave.'

Apparently Zinoviev's colleagues passed a resolution condemning the book as anti-Soviet without having read it. Zinoviev, of course, lost his job.

CHAPTER 11

BUKOVSKY EXPLAINS SOVIET PSYCHIATRY

The first real opportunity I had to have a proper discussion with Bukovsky after his arrival in London was at breakfast in the Hilton Hotel on 27 January 1977. He suggested the time and place, sounding a little like an IBM executive. I was disconcerted (and a little overawed) to find Winston Churchill MP also present when I arrived – he was apparently Bukovsky's 'minder'. Actually he was very pleasant and made no effort to guide the discussion or to interfere in any way. Nor did he try and hurry things along despite the busy schedule of meetings Bukovsky had lined up.

I thought Bukovsky looked over-tired, thin and pale and obviously in need of a good rest and fattening up. When I suggested this he remarked that he felt he had a duty to the prisoners he had left behind to work as hard as possible on their behalf while he could still attract the attention of the media. We discussed various strategies to help Dr Semyon Gluzman, who our Working Group had decided needed priority attention if he was to be released. He still had two years in the Perm camp and another five years of exile ahead of him.[*]

I asked Bukovsky to try and explain why the Soviet regime persisted in using psychiatry as a political weapon against its small dissenting population in the face of the revulsion this practice was causing abroad and the constant damage done to its image as a civilized country. Surely, I said, the flexibility of the Soviet legal system was such that anyone the regime wished to silence could be dealt with within its framework without the resort to practices which would have been regarded as barbaric even in the nineteenth century?

Bukovsky replied that it was virtually impossible to explain to

---

[*] Despite the most strenuous worldwide efforts on his behalf, he was made to serve his full sentence.

westerners how unreal Soviet life actually was. In a normal society, theories and conclusions grow out of the raw material of life. In the Soviet Union, the raw material of life is compelled to conform to the ruling theory.*

In the thirties, Bukovsky continued, Soviet geneticists were compelled to accept the theories of Lysenko who held that acquired characteristics were transmitted to subsequent generations because this suited the theory that human behaviour was entirely determined by 'objective reality'. Any deviation from the expected pattern could only be due to subversion or mental illness. The official line was, 'In a socialist society, there are no criminals, only sick people.' Religious believers, for example, must be suffering from a delusional state as religion had been 'objectively proven' to be false. So far as would-be emigrants were concerned, the 'objective superiority' of socialism over all other systems made them obvious candidates for the lunatic asylum. Understandably, the mechanistic ideas about human behaviour which derived from the experiments of the great Russian physiologist Pavlov tended to dominate psychiatric theory in the Soviet Union. As for Freud, with his emphasis on the individual and the importance of the unconscious, of instinct and of sexual drive, such ideas were rejected completely and to hold to them was as dangerous as to espouse the cause of capitalism or democracy.

But the abuse of psychiatry became most flagrant, said Bukovsky, because of the distorted definition of the concept of 'social dangerousness' which the authorities had developed. Of course, every psychiatrist accepts that some mentally ill subjects are 'socially dangerous', either because of the risk of self-inflicted injury, or the danger of violence to others. Rapists, child molesters and so forth may need to be kept under secure restraint. But in the Soviet Union a person could be classified (and frequently was) as 'socially dangerous' because he held ideas which authority considered dangerous to society. These might be religious, nation-

---

* In a perceptive essay, 'The Anatomy of Reticence', the Czech dissident playwright, Vaclav Havel, makes a similar point when he says, 'Our citizens live with the universal unspoken dread, "what new catastrophe are they planning for us with the best of intentions?" – utopianism they regard as simply more technical instructions for doing violence to the scandalous chaos of life and intensifying the pain.'

alist or reformist ideas. To be classified as 'socially dangerous' it was only necessary to advocate something the authorities did not approve of. Once this classification was made, a sane person could be restrained indefinitely. So far as the constitutional rights of the Soviet people were concerned, theoretically these were very considerable especially since the reforms introduced under Khrushchev, but Brezhnev summed up the reality when he said: 'The Soviet constitution confers great freedom on the people except the freedom to abuse freedom.' We agreed that Orwell could not have put the situation better.

Turning to the question of the use of psychiatry as a weapon, Bukovsky explained that this had many advantages – by declaring dissidents to be insane, all administrative hurdles, small as these might be, were jumped at once. It was only necessary to send an ambulance and some attendants in white coats and cart off the troublemakers to an appropriate clinic where the doctors knew what was expected of them. Friends and relatives were told, 'The doctors say he is mad and they know what they are doing.' Sometimes the victim's neighbours and friends, if not the family, were inclined to agree, 'He must be mad to say the things he says knowing what trouble it will bring on himself and his family.'

There was no need to collect evidence, no need for a trial; most important of all, the resultant detention was for an indefinite period until the thinking process had improved to the authorities' satisfaction. The victim was not entitled to legal representation and only a commission of three psychiatrists meeting about every six months could order his release. He had no rights of appeal to a higher authority (because there was none) or to any independent tribunal (no such tribunal existed either). In effect he became a permanent prisoner, detainable at the will and whim of the KGB.*

In most cases, the process of 'improving thoughts' did not take long because for a mentally normal person to be locked up in a mental hospital with real, and often dangerous, lunatics in conditions of terrible squalor, was quite unendurable to all except the most strong-willed. However, if a person's thinking did not immediately improve, the process was speeded up by 'treatment'

---

* Recently the KGB has allowed such a victim, Nikolai Baranov, to come to Britain after spending sixteen years trying to improve his thinking.

with drugs which had very unpleasant side effects. This really amounted to torture by drugs. That drugs were often given with purely punitive intent was revealed by the frequent use of a drug called 'sulphazine' which is injected; this is very painful, induces high fever, may cause convulsions and is totally without therapeutic effect. It has not been used in any Western country for fifty years.

Bukovsky went on to explain that the abuse of psychiatry was by no means a simple matter of dogma overriding common sense. There were many serious compounding factors, including the fact that there was no tradition of freedom of expression in Russia – subservience to authority was the norm and always had been. Thus anyone who defied authority was automatically suspect. At best he was conspicuously lacking in the instinct of self-preservation and in awareness of the precarious nature of his relationship to the authorities. Faced with the complexities and the manifold problems of Soviet society, both the authorities and the majority of the people tended to feel nervous when confronted with criticism. The almost universal reaction was to ask: 'Where will all this end?'

I certainly found my conversation with Bukovsky enlightening and refreshing, but also daunting. How could anyone from a secure background relate to a man who had undergone such extremes of human cruelty, endured them and emerged with his fighting spirit enhanced? I supposed that he must find us in the West insipid and naive – which, in many cases, we are.

CHAPTER 12

THE POT AND THE BLACK KETTLE: A Meditation from my Diary

4 March 1977

James Baldwin has written a moving open letter to President Carter in response to the latter's repeated attacks on the human rights record of the Soviet Union. The issues he raises are certainly of the greatest importance. First he sets out some of the most flagrant examples of the gross miscarriages of justice against American blacks – for example the cases of the 'Wilmington Ten' who were severely sentenced in 1972 for the crime of arson committed during a riot on the evidence of a young black who had been forcibly detained in a psychiatric hospital until he had agreed to give evidence against the accused. Later this witness recanted his evidence but the conviction went ahead. Then there was the case of the 'Charlotte Three' – severely sentenced on the evidence of witnesses who were subsequently found to have received large payments ($4000) for their cooperation with the prosecution. Baldwin continues: 'Too many of us are in jail, too many of us are starving, too many of us can find no door open to us.' (Touchingly he concludes: 'I love my country and you are the only President to whom I could have written this letter.')

That Baldwin is hardly a friendly witness so far as the US is concerned hardly needs emphasis – brilliant writer though he undoubtedly is. A black homosexual growing up in a pretty tough neighbourhood is unlikely to develop an objective view of white Americans whom he describes as the sickest and most dangerous people of any colour on earth today. His strongly evangelical nature doesn't help matters – one can smell the fires of hell scorching his pants. But Baldwin has a privilege denied to practically three-quarters of the world's population – he can attack his government verbally as strenuously and as often as he likes – and he can do so with impunity.

What he (and many others) are saying is that a nation with such a dreadful record of oppression of its black minority, with its acceptance of economic exploitation of other minority groups as well as many native-born Americans, has no right to point the finger of scorn at another country for alleged violations of human rights. What he does not say is that it is not official American government policy to condone the oppression of blacks – quite the contrary. The Federal Government has done a great deal to free the blacks from the restrictions previously imposed by state governments and others in the USA. I doubt whether, in any other country in the world today with a large black minority, blacks are making so much progress. It is one of the great (and few) achievements of our age. The Federal Government does not condone exploitation or poverty – it does what it thinks is best to try and alleviate these conditions. Of course it often fails, but its intention is to succeed.

Where the attitude of the Soviet Government is so open to criticism (in my view) is in its deliberate suppression of the right of the individual to express any personal opinion which does not accord with the official party line. Human beings are by nature diverse – not only in the way they are made but in the way they react and think. This is a biological phenomenon of the greatest value and importance. It is part of the process which leads to adaptation and survival. Its suppression is wrong morally and biologically. The Soviets justify their suppression of individual expression in the name of 'defending socialism'. But if it is morally correct for governments to defend dogma against individual dissent, then surely the Inquisition was right and should be reconstituted.

It is really grotesque that the architects of the Gulag (aided and abetted by the Baldwins of this world, who are numerous) assume the moral high ground so often and without challenge. And from their exalted perch they pour scorn on America (and the West) for its many, openly displayed, shortcomings – the widespread abuse of drugs, the acceptance of a disorientated, aimless youth culture, the street violence and crime, homelessness, the obscene disparities of wealth, the corruption and the rampant materialism. Every one of these evils is present in the Soviet Union, and is indeed increasing – what is lacking there is an industry which thrives on its display of everything tawdry, sensational and evil, never hesitating to use exploitation and distortion to increase the effect. In the USSR the media have a different role – it is not to titillate the jaded public but to bore it to death by the constant presentation of a sanitized version of events of such excruciating dullness that alcoholic oblivion remains the favourite route of escape for the audience.

Meanwhile the human rights questions which Baldwin and others pose are far from clear cut. The American constitution, and the Bill of Rights which underlies it, must be counted as one of mankind's greatest achievements. It doesn't prevent injustice or oppression, the exploitation of the weak, the aggrandizement of the unscrupulous and the feeding of the unlimited greed of the avaricious. But it provides, I believe, greater protection to the individual, irrespective of his or her race, colour or creed, than any other system. The thing that makes America most vulnerable to criticism is the tolerance and indeed support it gives to vicious regimes like those of Chile and Guatemala. The stock defence – 'the regimes are only local and temporary – look at Argentina' – is not really convincing. Certainly it must be agreed that the first duty of government is to maintain social order and to prevent the anarchy, which always leads in the end to the oppression of the weak by the strong; there are nevertheless parts of the world where archaic and manifestly unjust social systems are so entrenched that revolutionary violence seems to be the only way to achieve reform. The question is – can revolution result in freedom or is it always the precursor of a new tyranny which can only maintain itself by force? It is sixty years since the communist regime seized power in Russia and, despite emerging victorious from wars and other catastrophes, it is still ruled by thinly disguised naked force. Is this something inherent in communism? Are the inhabitants of a Marxist state doomed to be the victims of permanent tyranny? Who knows – but many people who should know believe the answer is yes.

1 April

I went to a meeting at the Conway Hall [the scene of many human rights campaigns over the years], to hear an address by Bukovsky. I think David Markham arranged it; he was looking ill at ease, even disgruntled. I think he is upset at the way Bukovsky has been taken out of his hands by people of whom, by and large, David doesn't approve.

In the beginning, after his arrival in the West, Bukovsky seemed to imply that he was not opposed to the communist regime in Russia; that what he and most other dissidents had been striving to achieve was respect for legality and human rights. He has now changed his position drastically – when a member of the audience asked him what he thought of the idea of 'socialism with a human face' he replied drily, 'The human face without socialism suits me a lot better.' In conversation with him later, he made it clear that he no longer believed in the possibility of real reform in any Marxist country and least of all in the Soviet Union. Marxism and humanism were incompatible ideals.*

* Another prominent emigré, Professor Kolakowski, a Polish philosopher now at All Souls, Oxford, expressed the same sentiments thus: 'Communism with a human face is as plausible as the possibility of fried snow-balls.'

CHAPTER 13

JOURNEY ON THE MOSCOW UNDERGROUND

It was early in March 1977 that I was approached by two young bearded men in London who asked if I could do something to help Petr Grigorenko get a medical certificate guaranteeing him medical treatment in London. They were intense, secretive and compelling. They were of Ukrainian origin, although English born (as they explained). Grigorenko was their hero and they represented a group of Ukrainian emigrés who were trying to help him.

Grigorenko, a former Red Army general and a war hero in his own right, was idolized by the Ukrainian community (I soon discovered) as well as by the Crimean Tartars whose cause (they had been expelled from the Crimea to central Asia by Stalin) he had taken up with relentless fury quite indifferent to the many difficulties his attitude caused him with Soviet authority. Grigorenko suffered from high blood pressure and arterial disease and, lately, from prostatic obstruction which required surgical treatment. Egil Nansen (the grandson of Fritjhof Nansen, the explorer and Nobel Peace Prize winner), himself an active participant in human rights activities in Norway, had sent Grigorenko an invitation to come to Oslo for the required treatment at the expense of a local committee but the letters had been intercepted by the KGB. Thus the authorities were able to claim that they had no objection to Grigorenko's proposed trip abroad provided that it did not involve any foreign currency charges to the state. This useful fiction was kept up while Grigorenko's medical situation deteriorated.

As it happened, I wanted an excuse to visit the USSR to meet several dissidents, especially Andrei Sakharov, and this appeal gave me an added incentive. Michael Scammell who was collecting material for his biography of Solzhenitsyn agreed to come with me, so jointly we enrolled in a Cook's tour. Six hours before the time of departure, Michael's visa was cancelled so I set off alone, armed with a medical invitation from a leading London teaching hospital offering an all expenses paid sojourn to Grigorenko. Apart from the loss of Michael's company and the great assistance his fluency in Russian would have been to me, I was looking forward to a meeting with Lev Kopelev which Michael had arranged.*

A day before my departure, my English Ukrainian go-betweens turned up with a beautifully hand-knitted pullover for Grigorenko. I suspected that somewhere within it there was probably a concealed message but I asked no questions. I had hidden the medical invitation (which had been officially notarized) in a special place which got it past a very careful examination of my person and baggage at Moscow airport.†

When I got to my hotel, The Metropole, I rang a friend (whom I shall call Yuri) who had been detailed to be my guide and mentor during my Moscow visit. He was the son of a well-known dissident. We arranged to meet outside the underground station in Karl Marx Prospect.

'How shall I recognize you?' he asked.

'I shall be wearing a very worried expression,' I replied.

'So will everyone else,' he answered.

'I will also have a green carrier bag from Harrods,' I said.

Yuri of course found no difficulty in spotting me and I guess my KGB tail did not either (if I had one; I never knew). I handed over the bag which contained six pairs of Levis (a better currency than gold coins in the Russia of that time) as well as a few practical sweaters from Marks and Spencer and some packets of chocolate and vitamins for transmission to prisoners in camps.‡

Yuri was anxious for news of his now rather numerous friends and relatives who had gone into exile abroad – he suggested the best and easiest way to talk freely was to ride the underground.

---

* Kopelev was the model for Rubin in Solzhenitsyn's *First Circle*.

† At that time foreigners caught with material which was not actually subversive were likely to have it simply confiscated and occasionally they might be sent back home. Things are a lot rougher now – it could involve a prison sentence or at least some very unpleasant days of interrogation by the KGB.

‡ Tanya Litvinov advised me on the best gifts to take. Ball point pens with a miniature ship floating in the barrel are highly prized by prison guards (mostly unsophisticated peasants). Gifts of this sort are given in exchange for privileges. Chocolate, vitamins, and basic medicines are also valuable currency, especially as they are not bulky.

Certainly it was the easiest way to avoid bugs. Nevertheless I checked everyone within earshot for evidence of KGB connections – a brown hat and a green raincoat is an ominous sign, I was warned. I did not see anyone conforming to this description.

As the whole world knows, the Moscow underground is a series of cathedrals connected by tunnels. It is very impressive. Although it is crowded, the muteness of the travelling public, their lack of expression and the tidiness does nothing to dispel the sacred atmosphere. One cannot even smell sweat. From time to time we changed trains and pretty soon I started to relax and enjoy myself and above all, to enjoy Yuri.

Yuri was a bright attractive young man, a good physicist who was doing well at the Moscow Institute for Experimental and Theoretical Physics when he made an unguarded remark in praise of Andrei Sakharov. Soon after, a search of his apartment turned up some typescripts dealing with the Helsinki Accords and non-compliance with its human rights provisions by the Soviet Union. This led to his dismissal from the Institute and he now eked out a precarious living giving freelance tuition to physics students.

I wondered what had made Yuri into an outcast – by nature, he was clearly neither a troublemaker, nor someone with a taste for attention seeking or self-punishment (which some dissidents certainly were). He talked simply and without rancour or bitterness. His sincerity was transparent, his evidence daunting. We talked about Soviet reality – not the controlled splendour paraded with astounding efficiency (and absolute lack of flexibility) by Intourist which is designed to dazzle tourists and usually succeeds. Nor did we speak of the cliché problems of the Soviet housewife – the endless queuing, and the double duty that involves working all day and tending house as well; there was no need to talk about the shoddiness of everything in the shops when it was all so self-evident. What he spoke about was the all-pervasive 'control', the need to obtain permission for every activity, the suppression of initiative and enterprise and, most bitterly, he spoke of the pervasiveness of sham and hypocrisy. Nothing official could be believed. Nothing bad could ever be reported. Only positive achievements made news. There had to be permanent sunshine, the workers in the fields always tackled their tasks with enthusiasm and laughter; if the lot of man was one of 'quiet desperation' this was never reflected in any of the official means of communication.

Cynicism is widespread if not universal – everyone is preoccupied with how best to survive and, if possible, beat the system. Bureaucracy ruled and bureaucracy was brutal, uncaring, insensitive and mendacious. It was also impervious to criticism and beyond reform.

Of course none of this was new – it just tended to make rather a deep impression when coming from someone caught up in the daily struggle. The contrast with the gay chatter and excited comments of my fellow Cook's tourists who had just come from some dazzling display at a museum or art gallery proved irksome indeed. But, in reality, the truth must lie somewhere between. There seemed no point in explaining that the exaggerated view of Western prosperity and freedom, so prevalent amongst educated Russians, is founded on a misapprehension, that there is drudgery and despair, poverty and corruption, hypocrisy and cowardice, control and manipulation in even the best of Western countries. Where the real difference lies is surely in the greater scope for the individual in most Western countries to express himself either for good or ill. He can finish up a dope head in some garbage dump or a contented, suburban, lawn-mowing, over-weight, baseball fanatic; the choice is his – or is it?

But we didn't philosophize – it wasn't the time or place and there was no point. All Yuri would say in explanation of the prevailing ethos was that Socialist man, Soviet style, had turned out badly. He was selfish, materialistic, narrow, lazy, dishonest and disillusioned. (Sounds like Baudelaire describing the French middle classes of the nineteenth century, I thought.)

But Yuri's instructions were to see that I met as many of the active dissidents still in Moscow as possible and our first visit was to the 'General'. No one, except of course Sakharov, is more admired by the dissident community (I was to discover) than Petr Grigorenko. It was easy to see why. He is a tall, charismatic figure. Despite his seventy years and severe ill health, he still carries himself in a soldierly way which commands instant respect. Grigorenko was once a sheet metal worker but after joining the Red Army he rose rapidly through the ranks until he reached the level of general. He fought bravely and was wounded several times. By 1961 he had begun to find himself in conflict with the Communist Party, of which he was a member, complaining that increasingly it was deviating from the principles of Marx and

Lenin. He was soon to discover that the Communist Party hates the true believer more avidly than the unbeliever. When his criticisms continued despite warnings to desist, he was expelled from the Party and ultimately stripped of his military rank (and pension). When he continued his defiance he was brought before a psychiatric commission and pronounced 'not-responsible' (i.e. insane) and incarcerated indefinitely in a special psychiatric hospital for the criminally insane. As Yuri said, 'They found him insane because what he said made too much sense.'

Although Grigorenko is a general to his fingertips, he is a gentle, understanding soul, sensitive and tolerant of human weakness. Yuri told me that, when he was finally released from the hospital, many of the inmates, genuine psychotic cases, wept. They loved this man who had shown them a kindness they never received from the hospital attendants. 'Good luck,' they called to him, 'we hope you will be back soon!'

It is little wonder that the Soviet psychiatrist, Dr Semyon Gluzman, revolted by the spectacle of this good and sane man being incarcerated in an asylum for the criminally insane, should react by compiling a medical dossier of the evidence which he managed to circulate. It so clearly established Grigorenko's sanity and the gravity of the mis-diagnosis that Gluzman himself was severely punished by being given a ten-year sentence.

Grigorenko, despite his infirmities, was always to be found in the foreground of protests at the trials of dissidents. He was most active in the cause of the Crimean Tartars who simply adored him. While I was in his apartment two Tartars (judging by their small stature and swarthy skin colouring) turned up to tell of some recent outrage. Grigorenko hurried them into the adjacent park for a conversation. Nothing of any consequence could be said in his apartment which was thoroughly bugged.

Grigorenko's wife Zinaida is also an engaging figure; heroic, humorous and animated, despite misfortunes which would overwhelm an ordinary mortal. Her first husband, her brother and sister and other family members died in the purges of the thirties. She has a mentally retarded son whom both parents clearly cherish – he said to me: 'I'm a monster but the man who killed my father [Grigorenko is his step-father] was an even bigger monster.'

In order to talk freely, Grigorenko took me into the park, watching the men seated at the benches with care – he knew by now who were his minders. He carried with him his large portable transistor radio from which he was never parted lest it be stolen or smashed by the KGB who were frequent visitors to his apartment. It was his only link with the free world. He showed me the jemmy marks and splinters on the lintel of his door where entry was forced during his absences.

I handed over the medical certificate which he later presented to the authorities.* It enabled him, in the end, to obtain permission to leave for the USA for medical treatment. He was allowed to take his wife and stepson and they all live now in New York.

My next visit was to a young mathematician, Volodya, and his attractive wife, Masha. Volodya was of course not working officially – one soon becomes aware of the enormous power that the state exercises over the individual when it is the sole employer. The courage needed to incur the inevitable penalty of compulsory dismissal defies imagination. But so does so much else I saw that day and during the remainder of my week in Moscow. How do you live in constant fear of the door bell? with the daily threat of arrest, confinement to some psychiatric hell, or exile to a place thousands of kilometres from loved ones, home and security? Where does this courage come from? What are the impulses which provoke it? How can we in the West, with the protection of the law, weak as this may sometimes seem, comprehend the lives of dissidents?

Later next night I was taken to a party. Many parties start about midnight; I wondered why. It was a subdued party – the recent arrest of Anatoly Shcharansky had made people aware of a severe tightening up against dissent. The wives of Alexander Ginzburg and Yuri Orlov were there. They were both attractive women and

---

* The case of General Grigorenko and his alleged 'creeping schizophrenia' aroused worldwide interest. After all, it is very rare for generals to concern themselves with the affairs of ordinary mortals even in countries where such activities are not restricted. For a general in the Red Army to do so gave credence to the view that he must be, to say the least, mentally abnormal. After Grigorenko arrived in the USA the Americans arranged for three psychiatrists of formidable reputation, Walter Reich, Alan Stone and Lawrence Kolb, to examine him independently. They each concluded that there was no evidence of previous or present mental illness. Other consultants from the Howard Medical School of the New York State Psychiatric Institute came to the same conclusion.

courageous beyond imagination. Both their husbands, founding members of the Helsinki monitoring group, were in prison awaiting trial. No one knew what the precise charges were but they feared that, as had happened in the Shcharansky case, fabricated evidence of criminal activities (working with foreign agencies, dealing in foreign currency and so on) would be introduced (it was). I suppose all prisoners' wives are moving, as they are the innocent victims of their husbands' misfortunes, but I found these two women especially affecting. They had an aura which I imagine arises from their sense of outrage and their determination to stand firm in defence of their men. Signs of self-pity were conspicuously absent.

Yuri Orlov had a scientific reputation which was almost the equal of Sakharov's. But he had been in conflict with Soviet authority on human rights issues for many years.* I had a long talk to his wife, Irina, explaining that an English barrister, John Macdonald, had taken up her husband's case (she already knew this) and that the widespread support he was getting from the world scientific community who had nominated him for a Nobel Peace Prize – an item she didn't know – made it probable that Orlov would not receive a heavy punishment – indeed, he might simply be exiled abroad. How wrong that prediction proved to be.

Irina Ginzburg had just returned from visiting her husband in a prison 160 kilometres from Moscow. She was forbidden to see him or to leave a parcel of food which did not comply with the prison regulations because it had not been purchased at the local shop. Her husband, who has tuberculosis, needed special food but not even basic foods are available in country stores. The cruelty of these decisions horrified and depressed me. They also reinforced my determination to do everything possible to help on my return home. Alexander Ginzburg is much admired by the other dissidents. An actively practising Christian, he had adopted his mother's Jewish surname to show solidarity with her and as a protest against the ever-increasing anti-semitism of the regime. Solzhenitsyn had appointed him to be in charge of what was called the 'Social Fund' (see Chapter 14).

---

* After serving a full prison sentence and years of exile he was released to the West as a goodwill gesture before the Iceland summit in October.1986.

About midnight Valentin Turchin, the Moscow representative of Amnesty International, turned up. He has been 'unemployed' a long time.* I thought him marvellous – humorous, intelligent, forceful, resourceful. The Soviet Union must have immense human resources if it can afford to discard people of this calibre.

By this time, I think I was coming to understand the motivation of people like Valentin, Volodya, Yuri and the others. They were the products of an educational process and a new generation which simply could no longer live within the stifling confines of an archaic ideology which does not work and cannot work and which has no relevance to the times in which they live and in which they wish to function. Education has liberated them from the grip of mediocrity, just as education has liberated women and is liberating blacks. Moreover the slave mentality which Stalinism produced is being bred out of them. They perceive the 'collective freedom' which socialism promised to be a sham. They will not settle for anything less than personal freedom. It may take a long time to achieve it, but they will do so in the end. The question is whether the struggle itself will cause such dissension that the world will perish in its struggle to be free. The ultimate freedom, of course, has always been death, but that is not an option in any biological sense. We must hope that common sense and the instinct for survival will combine to prevent the possibility of oblivion. But no one can guarantee such an outcome.

Yuri took me back on the last train. Many of the passengers were drunk and brawling and the pristine atmosphere of the underground was a little defiled; but actually I preferred it that way – at least it was human. The man sitting next to me was wearing a brown hat and a green raincoat – I was too tired to care.

* He was finally allowed to emigrate and now lives and works as a physicist in New York.

CHAPTER 14

EMIGRÉ POLITICS INTRUDE

Sometime in May 1977 Jane Ellis, one of the most dedicated of the Keston College* staff, rang me to discuss the possibility of starting a campaign on behalf of Alexander Ginzburg. I had already decided to try and do something for him after talking to his wife in Moscow. I had made the same promise to Mrs Orlov but soon found that John Macdonald had the Orlov case well and truly in hand. I considered that another committee would probably achieve very little – after all, there had already been a lot of protests at Ginzburg's arrest and even President Carter had made an appeal for his release – but there had not been much activity in the UK and I thought a short, sharp campaign led by a charismatic figure with media appeal might be worthwhile.

The obvious person for this role was Solzhenitsyn; Ginzburg had worked closely with him and had been the administrator of the 'social fund'.

This fund, consisting of Solzhenitsyn's royalties from *The Gulag Archipelago*, was used to help the needy families of political prisoners. The KGB claimed that monies came from the CIA, and that Ginzburg embezzled them for his own profit. He was also a currency smuggler, said the KGB, after planting some US dollars in his flat at the time of his arrest. In fact, the 'social fund', which amounted to $400,000, brought help to 600 prisoners in its first year of operation, and to 700 in the second year.

Negotiations with Solzhenitsyn, conducted largely by Michael Scammell, resulted in a refusal by him to come to London but an agreement that his wife would come on his behalf. It was a condition of the offer that a meeting with Mrs Thatcher (then leader of the opposition Conservative Party) was to be arranged.

---

* Keston College, founded by the Rev. Michael Bourdeaux, specialises in the study of religion, especially Christianity, in communist countries and is very active in helping those persecuted on religious grounds.

This was done and the relevant press and television people were alerted. A small public meeting was also to be part of the proceedings although experience had shown that it is mainly adverse political and media comment that worries the Soviets and may, at times, produce a satisfactory reaction.

The day before Mrs Solzhenitsyn was due to arrive, I received a telephone call from her. She expressed the Solzhenitsyns' great satisfaction with the efforts we had made to help their friend, but explained that they wished some changes in the arrangements. The first and most important was that no one, except a certain individual whom she mentioned by name, was to accompany her during her meeting with Mrs Thatcher. I did not feel it appropriate to enquire the reason for this request – it had been previously understood that Michael Scammell would be present, partly as interpreter and partly to represent the committee, but Mrs Solzhenitsyn rejected this suggestion point blank. The real difficulty, however, was that the person she nominated to accompany her was, to say the least, regarded in some emigré circles as 'dubious'. I did not understand what made him 'dubious': did he represent the NTS? Perhaps he had even more doubtful connections. At any rate I had no alternative, after consultation with Michael Scammell, but to explain that in these circumstances the Ginzburg Committee would have to dissociate itself from her visit, which should then assume a purely private character. I alerted Mrs Thatcher's secretary and the meeting took place, but what was discussed I never discovered. The media coverage was rather sparse and the whole episode left a bad taste.

It must be admitted that, if Russians have 'difficult' characters, exile rarely if ever does anything to improve matters. Exile is indeed a terrible punishment and burden to most Russians who seem, no matter how harshly or unjustly they may have been treated, to suffer great deprivation by being forced to leave their country. Many never seem to make a satisfactory adjustment even when their personal and financial circumstances have improved greatly which, in many cases, they have.

It is more or less a standing joke amongst those who work with Soviet emigrés that they have an unrivalled propensity to form themselves into mutually hostile cliques. Alexander Zinoviev says that five emigrés cannot constitute a threat to anyone – they will be too busy quarrelling amongst themselves. I have been to a party (at the Litvinovs) where there were approximately fifteen people and three mutually exclusive sets none of whom would speak to the other. I have never seen a group of emigrés mixed up together where they all seemed to be on good terms. But doubtless this does happen.

That Alexander Solzhenitsyn is a very difficult character is now beyond dispute. Apart from his special brand of religious mysticism and his fervent Russian nationalism, his character has been moulded by a system so oppressive and his experiences within it have been so horrendous that it is really beyond the imagination of the outsider to comprehend what he has undergone. Solzhenitsyn's obvious disillusion with the West is apparently compounded by the fact that through all his tribulations he was sustained by the belief that, in the end, the West would act to rescue the Russian people from the toils of communism. Clearly such a hope is entirely unrealistic. As a result, Solzhenitsyn has become convinced that the West is too flabby and spineless to put up a true defence of its freedom – that part of this spinelessness is a refusal to see the true face of communism, 'its savage structure and pitiless aims'. Too many people, he believes, are prepared to see the Soviet regime as simply an 'oriental distortion of a noble idea'. He feels that all the suffering of the Russian people, which might have at least served to warn and forearm the West, has been in vain. He attributes this failure to the mindless hedonism which has overtaken the people of the free world and reduced their willingness to defend freedom or God. He had hoped to find defenders of humanity in the West – instead he found wilful blindness and self-indulgence. But in truth, I think the root of Solzhenitsyn's problems with the West is the ineradicable grief he is suffering due to exile. He is far from being alone in this reaction.

It is the extraordinary fidelity of Russians to their native land which makes the regime's obsessive hostility to emigration so ridiculous. If they were to encourage emigration, it seems very likely that although there would be a flood of emigrants at first, that tide would soon reach a peak and then begin to ebb as disillusioned exiles sought to return home again. The present policy, under which the mere expression of a desire to emigrate comes close to being a punishable offence, is self-defeating. As with any form of prohibition, the prohibited activity is endowed with unreal attractiveness. Migration has always been part of the natural history of man's development. To impose a severe restriction on the freedom to migrate in a nation composed of so many nationalities is a dangerous absurdity. Not least of the dangers is that which derives from the unreal expectations of the 'outside world' which those excluded from it develop. In a world where ease and rapidity of travel increase daily, and where the allure of travel increases with it, a severely restrictive policy on freedom of movement must, in the end, collapse. The Soviet Union would gain rather than lose if it abolished all restrictions on travel. Indeed it will ultimately have no choice but to do so if it seriously intends to join the modern world.

PART TWO

The Fight Against
Political Psychiatry

CHAPTER 15

VICTORY AT HONOLULU

My conversations in the USSR had convinced me not only that a serious programme of repression was under way, but also that psychiatry was being used as an important weapon in that campaign. It was obvious that the dissidents themselves feared the prospect of psychiatric internment much more than that of a term in a labour camp. The authorities were well aware of the potency of the wepon they had to hand and clearly they had no inhibitions about using it. But the dissident community – not that it really was a community, more a disparate collection of individuals – did not take the situation lying down. In January 1977 a Working Commission to Investigate the Use of Psychiatry for Political Purposes in the USSR was established by a brave group of Soviet citizens in Moscow, acting within the rights and privileges granted to citizens of the signatories to the Helsinki Accord – or so they thought. This group will subsequently be referred to simply as 'The Commission' and most of its members will figure in the narrative which follows.

I decided to commit myself to the campaign against the political abuse of psychiatry. It seemed to me to be a dreadful abuse of state power, but also one which made the Soviet regime especially vulnerable as it so clearly contravened the ethical guidelines of medical practice which had universal applicability. I had already joined the Working Group on the Internment of Dissenters in Mental Hospitals which had been set up in London in 1971 and which Peter Reddaway had kept active (at the cost of sacrificing much of his time and energy) by providing a continuous stream of well-researched documentation and ideas for different initiatives to make use of this information. Others active in the group at that time were Dr Gerard Low-Beer, Dr Sidney Bloch and Dr Christine Shaw.

The three principal founders of 'The Commission' were V.

Bakhmin, a computer programmer, F. Serebrov, a skilled metal worker and A. Podrabinek, an auxiliary medical worker (or paramedic). The latter compiled a most lucid account of one hundred cases of psychiatric abuse which was subsequently published in the West with the title *Punitive Medicine*.* It is an extraordinary document considering the professional status of the author, for it would do credit to a fully qualified and experienced psychiatric research worker. 'The Commission' gave advice and assistance, where possible, to those threatened with, or actually interned in, psychiatric hospitals. It was careful to work strictly within the confines of 'Soviet legality': nothing was done secretly, every allegation was based on 'objective evidence' which was carefully verified and quickly amended if and when errors were found. Two Soviet psychiatrists, Alexander Voloshanovich and Anatoly Koryagin, assisted 'The Commission' in making psychiatric assessments.†

'The Commission' never claimed that every subject of its investigations was a mentally healthy person, but it did claim that many were so mildly ill that they could not be held to be either 'not responsible' or 'socially dangerous' on medical grounds. They reported that many subjects were confined to psychiatric hospitals involuntarily when they required no hospitalization at all, others were being compelled to receive treatment which they did not need. The views which the state authorities claimed made them 'socially dangerous' – the implication being that they were based on delusions – were in fact sincerely held and founded on conviction and proper contact with reality.

Ultimately, before it was disbanded by the imprisonment or exile of its members, 'The Commission' compiled 1500 pages of documentary evidence concerning the abuse of psychiatry for political purposes. This material was sent to the West where it was closely examined by independent authorities including Amnesty International, the Royal College of Psychiatrists and other national psychiatric bodies in Europe and America.

During the Spring of 1977, our own Working Group was active

---

* Karoma Publishers, Ann Arbor, Michigan, USA.

† Voloshanovich emigrated to the UK in February 1980 and joined our Working Group. He had been threatened with imprisonment in the USSR. Koryagin was imprisoned in February 1981 and released in March 1987.

in supporting both 'The Commission' and the many interned dissidents about whom it had provided details. There was not much we could do except write letters to the various authorities and send telegrams and petitions of protest. Many people might question the value of such activity – surely these letters finish up unread in some bureaucrat's wastepaper basket? Nothing could be further from the truth. Time after time, former inmates of prisons, psychiatric hospitals and camps have told us that the receipt of letters from abroad has been of immediate and great value in ameliorating their conditions. Every Soviet bureaucrat lives in dread of committing an offence which can be brought home to him. Paper is dangerous in the Soviet Union but it is also immensely important; nothing can be discarded – who knows what may happen? The knowledge that a prisoner is not alone but is under the scrutiny of 'silent voices from outside' is his greatest and usually his only protection.

Letters which come from scientific or official bodies have an even greater impact – they may never be answered but they are rarely ignored. The effect is subtle and cumulative. The Soviet government craves respectability – it knows how damaging its image of brutality and inhumanity is. After all, it has by such behaviour effectively cut itself off from the goodwill of communists and other sympathizers in many Western countries. The Soviet Union is to all intents friendless – and this is a problem they must solve, for it makes them feel more vulnerable than does the threat from missiles that only a madman would use.

The first real victory in the campaign against the Soviets' abuse of psychiatry was achieved in the most unlikely of settings – Honolulu, a place of tawdry hotels, swaying palms, honeymoon couples and over-fed American tourists thinking about practically anything except the problems of the Gulag. But it happened to be the site of the Sixth Congress of the World Psychiatric Association in August 1977 and, despite the most strenuous efforts by the Soviet delegation and its few satellite helpers, the psychiatric abuse issue was placed high on the agenda for debate. I had hoped to attend the Congress as an observer but was unable at the last moment to do so. Thus this report is based on information from my colleagues who did attend.

Just as he had done in 1971 before the Fifth WPA Congress in Mexico City, Vladimir Bukovsky sent a strong appeal to the participants of the WPA to take action against the abuse of psychiatry by their Soviet colleagues. By this time, Bukovsky had achieved a recognition that made it impossible for his appeal to be dismissed as just another attack on psychiatry by a disaffected person. (Psychiatrists are always being attacked for one reason or another and tend to become rather blasé or even hostile when non-psychiatrists raise ethical issues with them.) Bukovsky stated unequivocally that the abuse he complained of involved hundreds of cases, was increasing and could only be halted by 'unambiguous international condemnation'.

After much lobbying, a resolution was submitted to the Congress by the Australasian College of Psychiatry which, in brief, condemned the abuse of psychiatry for political purposes wherever it occurred. It called for the professional bodies involved to expunge the practice in the first instance 'in reference to the extensive evidence of the systematic abuse of psychiatry for political purposes in the USSR'. It is doubtful whether, since the end of the Second World War, the Soviet Union has been faced with such a humiliating accusation in an international context; a charge based purely on ethical considerations and framed by a body consisting entirely of professionals, many of them of considerable eminence.

The resolution was carried by a very slender margin – not because the delegates felt that the accusations were false or the evidence insufficient, but because of the very natural feeling that a milder approach which carried less risk of causing a rupture with the Soviet Union would be more appropriate. There was also a considerable body of opinion which held that the abuse issue was really a political matter and had no place on the agenda of a scientific society. Finally there was the widespread feeling, common amongst psychiatrists, that it is not the role of psychiatry to condemn human behaviour – only to analyze it and advise. In any case, if there were abuses of one kind in the Soviet Union, certainly there were other kinds of abuses, equally repugnant, elsewhere. Psychiatry is a glass house – it is no place for stone throwers.

But despite all these reservations, the World Psychiatric Association, representing practitioners of psychiatry throughout the civilized world, had come to recognize that the practice of psychiatry inevitably involves the weighing of ethical principles and that the time had come to try to codify the most important of these. Such a code (The Declaration of Hawaii) had been drawn up by a special committee established after the Fifth Congress in 1971. It was adopted by the Sixth Congress as a set of basic guidelines for the practice of psychiatry everywhere, irrespective of the differences in cultural, social, religious, economic and legal conditions that prevail among its disparate membership.

In brief, the code enjoins the psychiatrist to treat mental illness and to promote mental health to the best of his or her ability; to work in the best interests of the patient; to foster a close relationship with the patient or, if this is impossible, with the patient's relatives. Every effort should be made to foster a mutual relationship based on trust and agreement, the patient should be given as much information about his condition and the proposed treatment as possible, and the patient should, where feasible, be given the right to choose between alternative treatments or procedures. Compulsory treatment should only be given in the rare circumstances where the patient clearly cannot give informed consent. No other consideration except the medical needs of the patient should influence the management of the patient, and where any third party demands actions which are contrary to the objective evidence, whether that indicates an absence of psychiatric illness or a need for treatment, or which offends any other ethical principle, the psychiatrist should refuse to cooperate.Clearly, the Soviet practice of psychiatry breached these elementary guidelines in many instances.

One of the most impressive contributors to the debate which preceded the vote on the abuse issue was Marina Voikhanskaya. Russian born, bred and trained, she described four cases of gross political abuse of psychiatry with which she was personally familiar. She was strongly supported by Dr Boris Zoubok, a former Soviet psychiatrist now living in exile in the USA, who also witnessed firsthand the use of psychiatry for political purposes. Another effective speaker was Leonid Plyushch, a former victim of psychiatric repression, whose eloquent and dispassionate exposition left the delegates with no room for equivocation. The notion that this issue was something fomented by anti-Soviet elements was clearly untenable; the question was – what best to do?

In an attempt to forestall action, one of the Soviet delegates produced ten clinical reports of alleged cases of political abuse; it was claimed that the reports clearly indicated mental illness. However, five of the ten reports referred to victims who had subsequently emigrated to the West where they had been thoroughly examined by mental health specialists and found to be sane. They were Vladimir Borisov, Natalya Gorbanevskaya, Vladimir Bukovsky, Leonid Plyushch and Viktor Fainberg. This débâcle did nothing to strengthen the Soviets' position.

The actual vote, 90 for the resolution and 88 opposed (eight votes were invalid), was just enough to secure the passage of the resolution. The Soviet delegation criticized the voting procedure with considerable vehemence and not without some justification, for it was based upon the number of paid-up members of the national delegations (there was an upper limit of 30). Undoubtedly this was not a very democratic voting system and had the usual UN style voting method (one vote per member country) been in force it is likely that the resolution would not have carried. But it did carry and the consequences were to be far-reaching.

Having passed the resolution, the Assembly then decided to set up a special committee to examine the whole question of political abuse and it was given the task of reviewing and reporting upon cases of alleged political abuse submitted to it by members of the WPA. Its activities were in the end to prove important, even devastating.

CHAPTER 16

THE WEST SHOWS SOME MUSCLE

From 1978 to 1983 I was involved in efforts to ensure that the USSR complied with the WPA resolution which called for an end to the abuse of psychiatry for political purposes. To force the USSR to conform to something with which it did not agree was, of course, virtually an impossible task. But on this particular issue it was on shaky ground, and knew it. Our Working Group devoted most of its efforts to accumulating, assessing and correlating 'objective' evidence on the abuse issue, which came to us from multiple sources (mainly from within the USSR), and passing it on to the official bodies such as the Royal College of Psychiatrists who had by now taken the necessary action to assist the WPA in its unwelcome role as enforcer of ethics against a constituent member.

The fact that the WPA Congress had recognized the existence of the abuse issue in general and had named the USSR as the principal offender, meant that this was no longer one of several criticisms levelled at psychiatry from outside, but an officially agreed complaint which demanded action. The nature of that action was carefully spelled out. A special Review Committee was to be set up to which member countries could submit cases of alleged political abuse of psychiatry for evaluation by 'objective' experts. From the beginning, the USSR refused to recognize the legality of the Review Committee or to cooperate with it. But this attitude left it in a very weak position: the Review Committee had been officially established by the WPA membership, the USSR could not ignore its existence indefinitely and still remain a member of the WPA.

The membership of the Review Committee was carefully chosen; there were six members, each representing one of six regions of approximately equal size. Its chairman was Professor J. Y. Gosselin of Canada and the other members came from Czechoslovakia, Norway, Brazil, Egypt and India. Its procedures, formulated with the help of Anthony McNulty, Director of the British Institute of Human Rights, and a number of lawyers with experience of the minefield of international law, were carefully designed to conform to the best practice of international bodies.

The first case considered by the Committee was referred to it by the Royal College of Psychiatrists in August 1979. It concerned Yosyp Terelya, a Ukrainian nationalist and religious believer who had been found 'non-responsible' by the Serbsky Institute in 1972 after being charged with writing a tract regarded as 'anti-Soviet agitation and propaganda'. He was in fact already serving a long sentence for nationalistic offences in a labour camp at the time, but presumably it was thought that the camp regime was not severe enough to quell his spirit so something more 'therapeutic' was needed. He was sent to a 'special' psychiatric hospital for 'treatment'. From there he wrote an open letter to Yuri Andropov, then head of the KGB, entitled 'Notes from a Madhouse'. In it he detailed the horrors to which he had been subjected, describing them as so diabolic as to make the inmates of Dante's Hell envious. By the time his case was referred to the WPA he had served a total of six years in psychiatric hospitals; his case had also been examined in some detail by the Moscow Commission which believed that he was sane. He was married to a doctor who also regarded him as sane and who campaigned on his behalf, writing to the WPA Executive before the Sixth Congress in Honolulu appealing for help.*

In due course, 28 cases of alleged politically motivated psychiatric abuse were submitted to the Review Committee from the Royal College of Psychiatrists, the American Psychiatric Association, the Swedish Psychiatric Association and the West German, Japanese and Australasian Psychiatric Associations.

The dramatic nature of the Honolulu resolution, with its open condemnation of the USSR, created a furore which was widely reported in the international media. It also encouraged the media to draw attention to accusations of psychiatric abuse in the world outside the communist bloc. It is undeniable that occasional cases of psychiatric abuse with some political content are to be found practically everywhere. It is not only in the USSR that patients are brutalized and the dreadful discrimination against black South Africans needing psychiatric care has caused even the all-white

---

* He was released in 1981, and later sentenced twice to camp terms.

Society of Psychiatrists of South Africa to protest to their government. Meanwhile prison medical officers in Britain complain that far too many prisoners are clearly in need of psychiatric hospitalization and the practice of over-prescribing tranquillizing drugs in British prisons in order to keep obstreperous prisoners quiet is notorious. But, by and large, these allegations really amount to a question of medical malpractice; they are not inspired by political policies designed to suppress a dissident population – which is not to say that they are matters which should be accepted with complacency. They are a cause for reproach and show the need for reforms – none of which is more urgent than the provision of adequate after-care for the many schizophrenic patients now being released from institutions who have nowhere to go and no one to look after them properly.

In 1978 the Royal College of Psychiatrists and, shortly afterwards, the American Psychiatric Association established special committees to deal with the abuse issue. Our Working Group developed close links with both, especially the American committee, whose secretary, Miss Ellen Mercer, became a frequent visitor to Britain and a close personal friend. Her dedication to the abuse issue (in the face of considerable opposition from some sections of the APA membership) was noteworthy.

One of the most important and interesting initiatives in which the Working Group was involved concerned a visit to the USSR by Dr Gerard Low-Beer who was a member of our Group as well as a member of the special committee of the Royal College. A psychiatrist of great experience, he was also a fluent speaker of Russian and German and had been involved in the abuse question, in collaboration with Peter Reddaway, for a number of years. During his visit he was able, through the cooperation of 'The Commission', to conduct in-depth interviews with nine dissenters who had either been detained in mental hospitals for political reasons or who feared that such a fate soon awaited them. Using the narrowest of criteria of normality, Low-Beer concluded that, of the nine subjects, five were mentally completely normal while the remaining four had only minor abnormalities.* It is not

---

* I lunched with one of them, Evgeny Nikolayev several years later in Munich; I thought him a delightful character if slightly excitable. A German psychiatric commission headed by Professor W. von Baeyer came to a similar conclusion.

without interest or relevance that, since Low-Beer represented the College, his subsequent report which the Working Group published in an information bulletin, probably had an effect on the Soviet authorities. Only one of the nine, Vladimir Gershuni, was subsequently sent to a psychiatric hospital. He is still confined at the time of writing.

Throughout 1978 and 1979 the Working Group (and others) continued to write about prisoners and to gather information. Although it was difficult to measure, these activities certainly had some effect.* The arrival of Dr Alexander (Sasha) Voloshanovich in London in February 1980 greatly assisted the Working Group, whose ranks he immediately joined. Sasha had fallen foul of the KGB in August 1978, after giving a press conference in Moscow where he stated that he had examined 27 individuals, all of whom had either been detained as 'socially dangerous' because of mental illness, or were being threatened with such a diagnosis, and that in no case could he find evidence of mental illness. He made no claim that his diagnoses might not be in error – but he did state his opinion that none of the subjects deserved or required to be forcibly detained on medical grounds. Sasha gave his clinical notes, which were very detailed, to the Royal College and to Amnesty International for evaluation. They agreed with his general conclusions.

It is not clear why Sasha was given the option of emigrating when his colleague, Anatoly Koryagin, was jailed (and severely manhandled into the bargain); but it is probable that a letter from the Royal College of Psychiatrists inviting him to come to London as a guest lecturer conferred some degree of protection.

In June 1982, at the instigation of Lindsay Stewart (now Lady Avebury), refugee coordinator at Amnesty International and a dedicted fighter for human rights if ever there was one, I applied to the Ross McWhirter Foundation on behalf of Sasha Voloshanovich for the award of a Sakharov Scholarship. This award is for three years and includes annual payments of £1000. It is given to

---

* The results of a campaign on behalf of an individual can be very long in coming. It was in 1981, for example, that the Royal College decided to 'adopt' Nikolai Baranov, a victim of political abuse of psychiatry of a particularly distressing nature, but it was only in 1986 that he was finally allowed to emigrate to the UK.

suitable candidates reading for an English degree who have spent a large part of their lives in Russia or another Communist country. The closing date was only a few days away and Sasha, who was working as a nursing orderly, could hardly qualify as someone reading for a degree. But I felt that he had nothing to lose: he was very fed up with his lowly status and poor prospects and one of his principal grouches to me was that his situation interfered with his romantic aspirations – English girls, he believed, rightly or wrongly, attached more importance to a man's economic and social status than Russian ones.

At all events, Sasha was clearly lonely and discouraged and I felt that his best hope was to enrol in a course which could lead to his registration as a psychiatrist in the UK. I sent off a strong recommendation to the secretary of the Foundation and at the same time contacted Dr Bewley, then Dean of the Royal College of Psychiatrists and a powerful figure in the psychiatric world, especially in the group of hospitals around St Thomas's. He was enormously sympathetic and helpful and quickly arranged for Sasha to be enrolled in a suitable training course. Soon afterwards, Sasha was awarded a Sakharov scholarship and this proved an enormous boost to his morale to say nothing of his finances. Sacha completed a course of training in psychiatry and is now practising his profession in a London hospital. He is also happily married.

CHAPTER 17

INTERLUDE IN MADRID

One important initiative, which the Working Group took in conjunction with the Madrid branch of Amnesty International, was to arrange a press conference to present to the world media, gathered in Madrid in December 1980 for the opening of the review meeting of the Conference on Security and Co-operation in Europe (CSCE), its evidence concerning the continuing political abuse of psychiatry. The Helsinki Final Act had provided for periodic review meetings at which delegates of the participating nations would review the status of the various initiatives agreed at Helsinki.

Amongst these, of course, was the question of human rights. The Soviet Union, supported by its East European satellites, adamantly insisted this was purely an internal matter and not a topic for debate by outsiders. But unless they wished to abrogate the Helsinki Accord, which, clearly, they did not, they had no alternative but to listen to the comments (mainly critical) of the other members who claimed, justly, that human rights had become a legitimate topic for discussion in this forum. Our role was to provide delegates with properly organized documentation. Sasha Voloshanovich was able to present his unique personal experiences and other evidence came from Gerard Low-Beer, Professor Durand, a member of a Swiss group, and Dr Gerard Bles from a French group. I had the privilege of giving our data to a member of the British delegation, William Wilberforce, a descendant of the anti-slavery Wilberforce, who, I was told later, used it to considerable effect. I remember saying to him: 'Go to it. Slavery isn't over.'

The European media (though not the British press) made considerable use of the material we presented at the press conference and I believe it created an impression at the actual CSCE meeting (the meetings are confined to delegates) when the question of psychiatric abuse came up for discussion.*

Our mood at Madrid was fairly cheerful, though it was dampened by tragedy when Amalrik was killed in a motor accident while on his way to the meeting. Sasha and I took most mornings off to spend in the Prado. On the Sunday, we took a bus trip to Toledo; I doubt if I have ever seen anything more spell-binding than the cathedral with its treasures and the El Greco paintings. Sasha's enthusiasm was palpable; but at the end of the day he managed to lose me and when I last saw him he was chatting up a slim-waisted, dark beauty with shining eyes. I wished him luck as I caught the last bus back to Madrid.

I think by far the most stimulating experience I had in Madrid was the opportunity to sit in on several private, informal meetings at which Ambassador Max Kampelman, the leader of the American CSCE delegation, expounded the complex issues which underlay the Helsinki conference – especially the questions of 'détente', 'peaceful co-existence' and 'non-interference' in the internal affairs of sovereign states. Kampelman is a shrewd, expert negotiator with a wider grasp of socio-economic and historical influences which lie behind international relations than most of the American officials whom I have met. The latter often seemed to me to have limited insights and short-term objectives – Max is a very different kettle of fish.† No one (at least in my experience) understood better than he that between the East, led, and indeed dominated, by the USSR, and the West, led and probably equally dominated by the USA, there lies an unbridgeable ideological gulf centring on the rights of the individual. In the West the citizen

---

* Actually, the USSR seems to have created a rather clumsy trap for itself in its anxiety to gain some respectability in the eyes of Western public opinion. At this stage, nearly every communist party in Europe was at loggerheads with Moscow. The Soviet constitution, as revised by Brezhnev in August 1977, said, in part: 'The Soviet Union's relations with other states are based on observance of the following principles: sovereign equality; mutual renunciation of the use or threat of force; inviolability of frontiers; territorial integrity of states; peaceful settlement of disputes; non-intervention in internal affairs; respect for human rights and fundamental freedoms; the equal rights of people to determine their destiny; and fulfilment in good faith of obligations arising from the generally recognized principles and rules of international law and from international treaties signed by the USSR.' It would certainly be difficult to reconcile the Soviets' human rights record with these lofty sentiments – to say nothing of their behaviour in Poland and Afghanistan.

† He later became head of the US disarmament negotiating team at Geneva.

expects his or her government to protect and enhance those rights, while in the East it is axiomatic that the rights of the individual are at all times subservient to the needs of the collective. No one can believe that it is possible to reconcile these opposing points of view. But Kampelman and others argued, correctly in my view, that economic and other forces will inevitably compel, at first a moderation of the collectivist idea, and ultimately its abandonment. Needless to say, the other side believes exactly the reverse.

Negotiating with Soviet officials, Kampelman explained, has always been difficult. Their attitudes are pre-determined and not susceptible to reasoned argument. Moreover they are based on jargon-ridden, doctrinaire assumptions which usually make dialogue a frustrating and irritating affair. As another delegate expressed it: 'Negotiating with the Soviets is like dealing with a defective vending machine – talking to it isn't likely to produce the lolly, but sometimes a good kick produces an unexpected result.'

Consider two phrases which crop up in every official Soviet pronouncement on foreign policy – 'peaceful co-existence' and 'détente'. In the West we interpret these phrases in common sense terms to mean something like 'live and let live' and 'easing tension between nations'. But the Soviet understanding of the words is very different: to them all they really mean is that there should be no overt military action to achieve objectives while non-military ones such as the subversion of political parties, the destabilization of economies, the provision of support to all forces of 'national liberation' and the infiltration of centres of power, especially the media, with sympathizers, are available. A cynical Czech once told me: 'For the Soviets to proclaim their love of peace is like a harlot claiming she only fucks to protect her virginity.'

Thus, behind the constant parade of their peaceful intentions, the Soviets see nothing inconsistent with the 'Brezhnev Doctrine' of 1968 which proclaimed that any Soviet military action was justified to prevent a country opting out of the communist system. They were certainly prepared to take such action in Poland, and indeed did take it in Afghanistan, while at the same time proclaiming their peace-loving intentions to the world. In effect, the Soviet Union only recognizes international laws which have the effect of protecting or enhancing 'socialism'. (The same attitude of course applies to their internal laws.)

The impervious attitude which many, if not all, Soviet officials adopt in the face of reasoned argument is illustrated by a story I heard in Madrid. It concerned a Soviet delegate who was reproached at a meeting for making a statement which was clearly not true. He replied that the truthfulness of his remarks was borne out by the fact that he had made an identical statement at a meeting of the committee two weeks previously.

On other occasions, Kampelman openly said that while the US was cutting down the proportion of its gross national product which was devoted to military expenditure (he claims that between 1968 and 1981 American expenditure on arms declined by 25% in constant dollars) the Soviets were doing the reverse. This was the reality of 'détente' from the Soviet side and no amount of cultural and scientific exchanges (as provided for in the Helsinki agreement) would alter it. As a result, even when Carter was still in office, the Americans announced that they intended to increase their military expenditure and the Reagan administration of course greatly accelerated the process. Thus, at the end of 1980, it looked as if both sides intended to revert to the previous 'confrontational' policy. 'Détente', if it ever existed in reality, would go out of the window. I noted at the time that I saw all this totally mad military machismo as a psychological 'fix' for the Vietnam defeat. The communists made a terrible blunder when, simply to humiliate the Americans, they insisted on prolonging the war beyond 1968, when they could have got terms as good as the ones they achieved in the end.

CHAPTER 18

THE CAMPAIGN
GATHERS PACE

After the success of our intervention at the Madrid CSCE meeting in December 1980 Peter Reddaway took the initiative in organizing all the known groups working in Europe on the issue of psychiatric abuse so that they could speak with a united voice. Organizations like Amnesty have gained greatly from this cooperation although, of course, it has entailed much more organization, expense and, at times, compromise. But all of us felt a growing sense of urgency in the face of the increasing pressures on the members of the Moscow 'Commission', almost all of whom were by now in prison, camps, psychiatric hospitals or exiled, and the evidence that the numbers of dissidents being sent to psychiatric hospitals was, if anything, increasing.

Another important objective of the international group was to create an information bulletin to provide factual evidence, objective and verifiable, which official bodies such as the national psychiatric associations and the like needed if they were to make effective representations in such forums as the UN Human Rights Commission or, for that matter, the World Psychiatric Association. The International Association on the Political Use of Psychiatry (IAPUP) was set up in Paris on 20 December 1980. The founding members were the Swiss Association Against the Abuse of Psychiatry for Political Purposes, the UK Working Group on the Internment of Dissenters in Mental Hospitals, the Committee of French Psychiatrists against the Political Abuse of Psychiatry, the German Association against Psychiatric Abuse and the Dutch Podrabinek Fund. The last-named was led by Robert van Voren, a most important contributor to the fight for human rights. The dedication, courage and sheer youthful energy which he devoted to the cause is beyond praise. The formation of the Dutch group, which has done remarkably good work in the human rights field,* was originally inspired by Vladimir Bukovsky.

One of the most important assets which IAPUP acquired at this time was the active interest of an important West German journalist, C. E. Langen of the *Frankfurter Allgemeine Zeitung*, perhaps West Germany's most politically influential newspaper. He attended IAPUP committee meetings and reported the proceedings extensively – the only German journalist to do so. At this time the West German attitude to the Soviet Union was mixed; the Bear was very close and looked dangerous – many people did not relish the idea of provoking him. As a result, the West German Psychiatric Association, alone of those in Western Europe, was not keen to become involved with the abuse issue. Ethical considerations were not to their liking, especially if they seemed likely to involve a confrontation with the USSR. We did have, of course, important German supporters but not the support of a national association, though that did come later.

The effect of Langen's reports, some of which were also carried in French and Swiss newspapers, would be difficult to over-estimate. His articles were the sort of adverse publicity the USSR feared most, because they had influence in important quarters.

The first IAPUP *Information Bulletin* appeared in May 1981. It listed all the known current victims of psychiatric abuse and gave advice as how best to help them. It reported on the arrest of members of the Moscow 'Commission', including Bakhmin, Ternovsky, Podrabinek, Grivnina, Serebrov and, most disastrously of all, Dr Anatoly Koryagin who had taken the place of Voloshanovich as 'The Commission's' medical adviser. It also gave details of eleven new cases since our information bulletin of October 1980. The reports included details of the case of Viktor Davydov† and that of Alexei Nikitin, a coal miner who was to die tragically and prematurely after a period of harsh internment.

The first *Bulletin* set an extraordinary high standard for detail,

---

* Its greatest success was to protect Irina Grivnina against the KGB's attempts to intimidate her because of her involvement in the campaign against psychiatric abuse. It was largely due to the pressure of Dutch parliamentarians, mobilized by Robert's group, that Grivnina and her family were allowed to emigrate to Holland.

† Later to be a star witness at the Fifth International Sakharov Hearing in London in April 1985.

accuracy and helpful advice. It was completely non-polemical yet very compelling. (Subsequent *Bulletins*, of which there have been thirteen as at December 1986, have maintained this high standard and have secured an important circulation among human rights groups. This is largely due to the extraordinary care and attention devoted to them by the principal editors, Peter Reddaway and, later, Dr Christine Shaw.)

The growing worldwide concern at the widespread abuse of psychiatry for political purposes, especially in the USSR, which IAPUP *Bulletins* accurately documented, ultimately obliged the UN Human Rights Commission to take up the issue. We claimed, and provided evidence to support the allegation, that many individuals in the USSR (and a few in other communist countries) were being deprived of their liberty by involuntary admission to mental hospitals for political and not medical reasons, and that they were being subjected to compulsory, inappropriate and unneeded medication which, at times, amounted to torture. These were very serious charges and it was no longer possible for them to be ignored. In November 1981 the UN General Assembly resolved to institute a far-reaching investigation into the law and practice governing the care of the mentally ill, with special emphasis upon the question of involuntary incarceration, indefinite detention and the compulsory administration of medication. The question of the safeguards required to protect people detained involuntarily were, in particular, to be studied and guidelines were to be established.

By the end of 1981 it had become obvious that the Soviets had no intention of responding to the appeals, which had come from many quarters, to reform the abuses of which they stood accused – and, to the satisfaction of most competent observers, had been proven guilty. The strong ethical convictions of the President, Professor Kenneth Rawnsley, and Vice-President, Professor Peter Sainsbury, led them to put a resolution to the general assembly of the Royal College of Psychiatrists on 20 November 1981 which read as follows:

It is resolved that the Royal College of Psychiatrists request that the General Assembly of the World Psychiatric Association at its meeting in Vienna in 1983, considers the following resolution:

'In view of the well documented evidence of the continuing systematic abuse of psychiatry for political purposes in the Soviet Union since the General Assembly's resolution of September 1977 to "renounce and expunge these practices" and the failure of the All Union Society of Neurologists and Psychiatrists [the official title of the Soviet psychiatric body] to cooperate at all with the WPA's Review Committee on the Political Abuse of Psychiatry in its investigation of various complaints from the Royal College and other member societies of the WPA, this General Assembly resolves that the All Union Society be expelled from the WPA until such time as the All Union Society can show that the political abuse of psychiatry has been brought to an end.'

This resolution was carried by an overwhelming majority. To say that it was a bombshell would be an understatement. For it put the world psychiatric community on notice that one of the most important national psychiatric bodies was not prepared to sit back and allow the abuse issue to become bogged down by endless procrastination and evasion either from the AUSNP or from the WPA. It was, in fact, an ultimatum with a deadline – the Vienna Conference of the WPA in May 1983 – and a declared aim – the expulsion or the reform of AUSNP. It also had added impact because of Britain's special reputation for fairmindedness, restraint, and political 'balance' in the field of diplomacy and world politics.

The response of other WPA members was not long in coming. The Danish Psychiatric Association adopted an identical resolution with members voting 160 for and 26 against. Soon afterwards, I had a meeting with the leaders of the Australasian College of Psychiatry who affirmed that their support for the motion could be assumed (it was later confirmed officially). On 25 June 1982 the American Psychiatric Association's Board of Trustees (its governing body) adopted a similar resolution, except that it substituted 'withdrawal of membership' for the harsher 'expulsion' demanded by the Royal College. On 23 September, the Swiss Society of Psychiatrists endorsed the Royal College's resolution as did two of the four French psychiatric bodies.

The West German Psychiatric Association expressed sympathy with the resolution but voted to reserve its position until there was further evidence of Soviet non-compliance; this 'wait and see' attitude reflected German hesitancy in involving themselves in confrontations with their neighbours to the east. The Canadians refused to commit themselves in advance, largely, it was felt, in order to demonstrate their independence from the US, but it was clear that if it came to a showdown, they would support the Royal College's resolution. The support of the Dutch and the Norwegians was soon forthcoming also. Thus, by the end of 1982, there were already enough votes committed to the resolution to ensure the expulsion of the AUSNP unless the latter was able to show convincingly that it intended to comply with the demand to expunge the practice of abusing psychiatry for political purposes.

The way in which the campaign against the AUSNP had developed among the WPA membership, and the certainty that, if the matter were put to the vote, the AUSNP would simply be expelled or at the very least, have its membership 'suspended', created a serious problem in the Kremlin. The expulsion of one of its national scientific institutions from an international body on ethical grounds would represent an extraordinary humiliation and it would also set a precedent which could have serious repercussions in other international bodies where the Soviet Union was represented, including the World Health Organization. The politicians ordered the bureaucrats of the AUSNP to do something to head off the danger. Some conciliatory approaches were made to the WPA secretariat and there was even a suggestion that the WPA should arrange for a commission of impartial psychiatrists to visit the USSR and see the situation for themselves. But similar missions had taken place in the past and it had become clear that the Soviets were expert at arranging such events in order to display the best and conceal the worst, and experience suggested that such a mission would be so confused by flattery, charm and apparent frankness that its members would either be unable to reach agreement or would content themselves with muted comments that fell far short of outright condemnation. The British therefore laid down two conditions for such an inspection which would have made effective concealment impossible:

1. The patients to be examined were to be nominated in advance by the delegation.
2. The patients were to be interviewed in the places where

they were normally detained and in the presence of members of their families; the interpreters would be brought from outside the USSR by the delegation.

These conditions raised the question of 'verification', a key issue in so many negotiations with the USSR, in the clearest way. The Soviets claim on every possible occasion that they are reliable treaty partners, but when faced with a demand that their compliance with their commitments should be subject to verification, they baulk. The British demands thus forced AUSNP to confront an issue which is central to high Soviet policy. Nevertheless, they seemed to come close to accepting the conditions before, presumably on orders from 'above', they pulled back and delivered a bombshell of their own.

CHAPTER 19

THE SOVIETS ADMIT DEFEAT

On 10 February 1983, the President of the World Psychiatric Association, Professor P. Pichot, who had been desperately trying to serve out his term in what is in fact a rather prestigious office without getting too deeply involved in any unseemly squabbling, received a rude shock. It took the form of a vituperative letter from the AUSNP, signed by every member of its praesidium, which stated that the AUSNP was forced to resign from the WPA because the leadership of the WPA in conjunction with certain national societies had collaborated in a politically inspired slanderous campaign alleging that psychiatry was being used in the USSR for political purposes. The Americans and British were accused of orchestrating this campaign.

The letter contained several quite misleading accusations, the most important being that the president of the American Psychiatric Association had invited members of the WPA who had information concerning the political abuse of psychiatry to pass this to their respective foreign ministries in order that it might be made available to the Human Rights Commission of the United Nations which was considering the question. This was a perfectly reasonable request – our own Working Group and IAPUP had been doing just that for some time – because there were few other reliable sources of information for the UN delegates to work from. The Soviets chose to regard this letter as libellous (because it implied that abuse of psychiatry was going on in the USSR) and an unwarranted incitement to interference by a governmental body with a non-governmental scientific organization. They entirely ignored the fact that the Human Rights Commission is specifically empowered to receive testimony from accredited non-governmental bodies.

The letter went on to state that many Western psychiatrists had had opportunities to examine alleged victims of psychiatric abuse in the USSR, and that none had ever expressed reservations (quite untrue) and that most of the so-called 'sane' victims of political psychiatry who had emigrated to the West were receiving psychiatric treatment including hospitalization. This was also quite false. I followed up nearly forty such cases and although there were some with psychiatric problems, mostly mild, virtually none had problems beyond those to be expected as a result of emigration alone. One case of suicide was known. Of ten former victims who I was able to spend considerable time with on more than one occasion, none could be called mentally ill.

The letter accused the WPA leadership of fostering a divisive, politically inspired campaign of slander against the Soviet Union when, in truth, they had done everything possible to avert it.

Needless to say, the announcement of the resignation which the Soviets made officially to the press on 10 February aroused widespread comment and considerable concern. It was the first time that any Soviet organization had, in effect, been forced to resign from an international body on clearly ethical grounds – nobody believed the official explanation to be anything but a smokescreen. The resignation simply pre-empted inevitable expulsion and was a humiliating admission of guilt. Certainly, it was clear that the powers that be (and at this stage it was not clear exactly who these were: Andropov was at the head, but was too sick to be in control) in the USSR did not think they could defend themselves successfully in a debate on the abuse of psychiatry which was inevitably going to figure large on the agenda in Vienna.

On behalf of the Working Group, I issued a statement which said, *inter alia*:

> The Working Group sees the move as a tacit admission that political psychiatry has been practised in the USSR and as a sign that the new Kremlin leadership may have taken the first steps to abolish this perversion of medicine. The Group believes that the process of abolition will take place gradually and unobtrusively and will take some time as structural and personnel changes will be necessary. It hopes that when the process is complete, the AUSNP will be re-admitted to the WPA.*

* Although the evidence is not complete, there are good grounds for believing that this assessment was correct.

On 12 February, the Soviet health ministry published an official comment on the resignation claiming this time that it was due to 'disagreements with other member countries over definitions and concepts of psychiatry'. Some members of the world body took a 'non-objective' approach to psychiatric problems, the spokesman added. I wrote a detailed reply to *The Times*, pointing out that this was simply an ingenuous attempt to hide what in fact was one of the most humiliating episodes in recent Soviet history and that the leadership must recognize this to be the case and allow the many well trained and ethical psychiatrists in the Soviet Union to resume unfettered control of their profession when they would, and should, rejoin the world body where they rightly belong.

This turn of events caused considerable discussion and perturbation in psychiatric circles (and elsewhere) worldwide. On 19 February 1983, *The Lancet* published a detailed article which I had prepared to explain the background to the dispute between the Soviet Union and the world psychiatric community. In the preamble I gave it as my opinion that the resignation of AUSNP from the WPA, rather than hindering the much needed and desired reduction in tension between the superpowers, would lead to the reverse – that it represented a highly significant victory for human rights which, in the long run, would do good. I concluded that, after a decent interval both to allow time for face saving and the clearance of the bottlenecks inseparable from the Soviet system, the bureaucrats who had led the Soviet psychiatric community into this humiliating position would be replaced. A new generation of younger, better-trained and less doctrinaire doctors, of whom there was no true lack in the USSR, would then abolish the abuses and restore Soviet psychiatry to its rightful place in the world scientific community.

My claim that, in adhering to a strong ethical stand, the world psychiatric community had achieved a victory for human rights was severely criticized from a number of quarters especially in the USA. Many important American psychiatrists were angered, others were concerned, and still more were confused that matters had been driven to the point where the Soviets had been given no real choice but to resign. Were the accusations justified? Did any country feel free to accuse another of violating human rights when its own record hardly bore scrutiny? Surely dialogue was better than silence? ('Expulsion is the best form of dialogue,' said

Bukovsky with typical but accurate bluntness.) Some advocated that the AUSNP should be politely asked to come back – it's all a misunderstanding, let's work it out together. But the debate was not one-sided. Stalwarts like Professor Harold Visotsky, Chairman of the Committee on Abuse (of the APA) poured scorn on the appeasers. Meanwhile the plausible Marat Vartanian continued to present the best possible face of Soviet psychiatry to the world. In a report broadcast from Moscow Radio on 24 March, 1983, he said:

> The slanderous campaign waged against the Soviet Union by the West is part of the anti-communism crusade declared by the Washington administration. So far as so-called sane dissidents being forced to receive psychiatric treatment is concerned two, Alexander Volpin, now in the US, is under constant psychiatric supervision [quite untrue] and Natalya Gorbanevskaya who emigrated to Great Britain [she did not, she went to France] required the services of a psychiatrist on several occasions. [Gorbanevskaya assured me that since her emigration, and indeed before it, she has never needed psychiatric assistance.]

Despite these blatant untruths, the amount of adverse comment which was expressed about the policies which had forced the AUSNP's resignation had a somewhat dampening effect on me (and no doubt on others involved in the question). But I was immensely reassured to receive a letter from Tom Stoppard who mentioned that he had read my *Lancet* article (his wife is a doctor and a *Lancet* subscriber) and that he agreed with my conclusions absolutely.

CHAPTER 20

THE TRAGEDY OF ALEXEI NIKITIN

In order to illustrate the sort of problems which we faced and the discouraging failures we so often had to endure, it is, perhaps, worth including a detailed description of one of the cases of psychiatric abuse in which our Working Group took a special interest.

Alexei Nikitin was born in 1937, the son of Ukrainian peasants. He worked first as a coal miner and then as an electrician in the coal mining industry. He first fell foul of Soviet authority when, after meritorious service in the Soviet Navy, he returned to his job as an electrical tradesman in a coal mine in the Donetsk area. From 1965 onwards, he became increasingly aware of discontent among the miners; this was due to many abuses, but especially the unfair distribution of bonuses, the allocation of the most lucrative coal faces to privileged workers (who paid for the privilege), discrimination and bribery in the allocation of housing and a lack of concern about unsafe working practices in the mine.

When repeated personal complaints were ignored, he took the initiative in leading a deputation of 130 fellow miners to complain to the mine Director. This entirely lawful action led to immediate and severe reprisals as well as to dismissal of the complaints. Nikitin was down-graded and then dismissed from his job and from the communist party. A subsequent inquiry did, it is true, lead to the dismissal of the mine Director, and in 1971 the unsafe electrical wiring in the mine, of which Nikitin had complained, caused a fire which resulted in seven deaths. But neither of these events helped Nikitin. After two years of making futile efforts to achieve re-instatement, Nikitin decided to seek publicity for his case by delivering a file of documents about his treatment to the Norwegian embassy. But he was intercepted and charged with disseminating 'fabrications defaming the Soviet State.' After a pre-trial examination, he was declared 'not responsible' and admitted to the Dnepropetrovsk Special Psychiatric Hospital where he was forced to take a psychotropic drug, 'majeptil', which is a potent tranquillizer. When he objected to the treatment he was told, 'You were brought here forcibly and you will be treated forcibly. If you do not take this pill, you will be bound and injected with it.'

Nikitin gave a detailed account of the conditions in the hospital ward where he was detained to an American journalist, Kevin Klose, who published it in his book, *Russia and the Russians*.* The description, which would fit an eighteenth century lunatic asylum, closely matches that given to me by Petr Grigorenko who was held in similar hospitals. The orderlies in the psycho-prison, who were for the most part convicted criminals, behaved with great brutality; any hint of resistance or disobedience was met with ruthless punishment. 'An unguarded laugh or even a cry of despair could bring reprisals. The orderlies bullied and provoked hoping for an opportunity to exact punishment.'

Nikitin was repeatedly injected with neuroleptic drugs (thorazine and haloperidol) as well as sulphazine, a therapeutically useless drug with intensely painful side effects which is really given as a punishment. Nikitin was officially diagnosed as a case of 'psychopathic personality' – an elastic term which embraces anti-social attitudes, a lack of concern for others, lack of guilt or remorse and, often, a tendency to violence. That Nikitin did not display any of these symptoms can be easily shown. He never advocated violence and was never himself violent, he was popular with his fellow workers (which psychopaths rarely are) and even after he had become a marked man, under the constant scrutiny of the KGB, his workmates went out of their way to show respect and solidarity with him thus risking their own safety. No criminal charge was ever brought against Nikitin, no doubt because it was administratively so much easier to keep him in hospital whenever the authorities wanted him restrained.

Nikitin was released from the hospital in 1976. He was unable to get a regular job because of his record so he went to the Norwegian embassy and asked for political asylum. But he was told that this could only be arranged from outside the USSR and was escorted back into the waiting arms of the KGB who returned

* W. W. Norton, New York, 1984.

him to hospital where he remained until 1980. After his release he went to Moscow and managed to arrange a psychiatric assessment by Dr Anatoly Koryagin (on behalf of 'The Commission'). Koryagin described Nikitin in these terms:

He shows strong-minded independence, an acute social conscience, a genuine sensitivity to the needs of others, and a dedication to improving the lot of the citizens of his homeland. His optimism is infectious and engaging; he suffers from no psychiatric illness or personality disorder and there is no evidence that he ever had any of these conditions. His admission to psychiatric hospitals should be considered totally unjustified.

It was in December 1980 that Nikitin happened to meet Kevin Klose, the Moscow correspondent of *The Washington Post*, and David Satter of the *Financial Times* in the flat of Felix Serebrov. This was the time of the Solidarity crisis in Poland and the two journalists had gone to see Serebrov in the hope of getting information about the likelihood of similar trade union activity in the USSR. Since Nikitin was currently involved in a campaign to establish a free trade union for coal miners, he invited the correspondents to accompany him to his home in Donetsk to see for themselves the conditions under which the coal miners were working. Klose describes Nikitin thus:

A balding 42 year old Russian with a fleshy nose, cornflower blue eyes set wide in his round face, with a mouth which held numerous steel capped teeth, his broad hands were calloused from years of manual labour and he had the rough and ready humour of his peasant forbears. A sturdily built Russian Everyman, without privileges or *blat* (pull) he was thoroughly at home in the pungent hard class world of minimal comfort known to the Soviet proletariat.

The correspondents accompanied Nikitin on the train to Donetsk and spent three days there, being shown round by Nikitin and dodging the police who were looking for him. Five days after the journalists left, Nikitin was picked up and returned to the psychiatric hospital. Klose later described this encounter to me and added that he met Koryagin personally (at Grivnina's house) and was thus able to confirm the latter's conviction that Nikitin was an absolutely sane man. David Satter also told me that he had formed the same opinion.

Early in 1982, the Working Group decided to try and help Nikitin through the intervention of the National Union of Mine Workers, a Union with strong sympathies with the USSR which, we believed, the latter would not wish to impair. The Secretary of the North Wales Area of the NUM, Mr Ted Mackay, wrote a detailed account of the Nikitin case which was published in the *Journal* of the NUM in March 1982 and the President of the NUM, Mr Joe Gormley, wrote to his counterpart in the USSR seeking information but received a mendacious reply from an official called Srebny which alleged, falsely, that Nikitin had committed criminal acts and had been tried and convicted for these. David Satter obtained a copy of this letter and in August 1982, he wrote to Arthur Scargill, who had succeeded Gormley as President, as follows:

I was a friend of Mr Nikitin and the last Westerner to see him before he was seized in December 1980. In fact it was my eagerness to write about the conditions of Soviet coal miners and Mr Nikitin's willingness to help me, which, I believe, led to his arrest. I feel you should know that Mr Srebny's letter contains not a truthful fact. Nikitin was not expelled from the Communist Party because of 'scandalous behaviour in rela- tion to his wife', but because he led a delegation of miners who protested against the arbitrary cancellation of bonuses for extra coal which was mined on Sundays. He did not beat his wife (as alleged) but divorced her after she wrote a denunciation of his activities to the local authorities at their request. She justified her action by saying she thought it would result in mercy being shown [it didn't]. Nikitin claimed his wife always opposed his actions on behalf of his fellow miners, saying, 'why don't you keep quiet and steal like the rest of them?'

Between April 1980, after Nikitin's release from the hospital, and December 1980, Satter met Nikitin many times in Moscow to discuss his life and the situation of the coal miners which communist propaganda routinely portrays in glowing terms. According to Nikitin, their true conditions are often appalling and Satter (and Klose) observed this at first hand. It was apparently these meetings which caused Srebny to state in his letter, 'in the eight months when not in confinement, there was no change for the better in Mr Nikitin's condition.'

To his credit, Mr Scargill did not accept Srebny's report without demur – in reply he said, *inter alia*, 'I must confess I find your explanation difficult to accept in total. I conclude by hoping that no miners or workers in the Soviet Union have or will be subject to the sort of treatment alleged of Mr Nikitin.' There the matter rested until January 1983, when Geoffrey Seed, an independent television producer who was making a film on the treatment of dissidents in the USSR, contacted Mr Scargill to enquire what action the NUM had taken in response to a direct appeal for help which it had received from Nikitin. Scargill dwelt on what he had done about the appalling conditions of miners in Bolivia and Chile, and would not offer any assistance to Nikitin beyond a letter the NUM had written some time before to the Soviet Coal Miners Union.

On 17 April 1984, I received a telephone call late at night from someone whose name I did not know and did not record, telling me that Alexei Nikitin had died. I was deeply shocked by the news but felt that independent confirmation was needed. I therefore rang David Satter who was in Paris. He had had no news, but within an hour he had obtained unequivocal confirmation of the sad fact from a source in Moscow. The details were vague. It was said that Nikitin had become ill in May 1983, had been found to be suffering from cancer of the stomach. He was allowed to go home where he died. No one except the KGB really knows the details. But it is certainly true to say that the death toll among imprisoned dissidents is very high: a reflection of the harsh conditions in which they are held, the inadequate diet, over-work and absence of proper medical care.*

---

* The latest, and most scandalous, death of a camp prisoner unjustly held is that of Anatoly Marchenko, one of the many heroes of the human rights struggle in the USSR. While serving a ten-year sentence for 'anti-Soviet propaganda' in Chistopol prison, he went on a four-month hunger strike and died early in December 1986. He was 48 years old and had spent twenty of these brief years in

CHAPTER 21

THE MARTYRDOM OF
DR ANATOLY KORYAGIN

If I was asked to select just one example in order to justify my
conclusion that the Soviet system is a brutal and repellent one
which should be criticized and condemned by civilized men and
women everywhere, then I would be content to rest my case on
the regime's treatment of Dr Anatoly Koryagin. For, in my
opinion, his experiences alone must call into question the claim of
the present Russian government to be included amongst the truly
civilized nations of the world.

Anatoly Koryagin was born in 1938 and has a wife and three
children. He graduated in medicine in 1963, and worked as a
psychiatrist until 1970, when he undertook post-graduate studies
in the Research Institute for Neurology and Psychiatry in Kharkov. His research thesis, which he successfully defended in 1972,
dealt with an obscure but important clinical aspect of schizophrenia. This is a significant point, for it not only establishes that
Koryagin was a well-qualified psychiatrist, but also that he had
special experience with schizophrenia, the topic which was later
to lead him into conflict with the authorities. He has held a
number of important medical posts, including that of deputy head
doctor of the Krasnoyarsk Psychiatric Hospital and consultant to
the Kharkov Regional Psychiatric Centre.

In 1979 he began to give psychiatric advice to the Moscow
'Commission' regarding the mental state of individuals whom the

<hr>

footnote continued

camps and prisons. Long periods of malnutrition had made him almost blind but
he had written a moving account of his experiences and of camp life entitled 'My
Testament' which made a deep and painful impression in the West. He had been
given a chance to emigrate (to Israel) but had declined, partly because he was not
Jewish, but mainly because of his dedication to the fight for human rights in the
USSR which he felt could only be effectively carried on within its borders. During a
period of freedom, he married the former wife of Yuli Daniel. Marchenko's death
was particularly tragic as it seems very probable that, after Sakharov's release from
exile, Marchenko would have been freed also.

'Commission' considered to have been incorrectly diagnosed as mentally ill or threatened with psychiatric internment on purely political grounds. He examined sixteen subjects (with their permission) and subsequently sent a detailed report of his findings to *The Lancet*, the oldest and most widely quoted medical journal in the world. Koryagin's report was published on 11 April 1981 under the title 'Unwilling Patients'.

He concluded that none of the subjects suffered from any mental illness, psychic defects or psychopathy, either at the time of his examination or previously. Nor did they exhibit evidence of a predisposition to mental illness: on the contrary, most showed evidence of strong personality, enterprise, energy, leadership and a desire to communicate. Since childhood they had been quick to learn, interested in achievement and determined to overcome difficulties. Many had diverse interests, sound and logical judgement, adequate emotional responses and realistic plans for the future. Despite the obvious superior quality of these subjects, they had all come into conflict with Soviet authority and been labelled as mentally ill. Koryagin noted that none of the subjects had sought psychiatric assistance nor had their families requested it.

The psychiatric examination and subsequent disposal had been initiated by the state authorities acting on charges related to 'anti-Soviet' articles of the Soviet penal code. The main abuses concerned religious beliefs, a desire to emigrate, or complaints about the administration (so-called 'reformism'). Some of the detentions were clearly intended to prevent the victims taking advantage of the media attention that would be directed at the Soviets on occasions such as the visit of President Nixon in 1979 and the 1980 Olympic games. Many of the subjects were compulsorily confined on the grounds that they were 'socially dangerous'; yet they were not dangerous to themselves, their families or associates, being invariably non-violent. It was their ideas which made them dangerous to the social system – that is, to the state. Koryagin concluded that: 'They were all classified among the mentally ill because they said or did things which, in our country, are considered "anti-Soviet."'

Of the sixteen subjects, 70% had been diagnosed as 'psychopathic' and 30% as schizophrenic. But whatever the diagnostic label employed, it almost invariably included a reference to 'paranoid tendency', a phrase which has a rather special meaning in Russia where, as a doctor had noted on one of the case records, 'no normal person can be opposed to the workers' and peasants' state'. Despite the fact that they were so ill as to require compulsory incarceration a number of the subjects were given no treatment (the term 'wall therapy' was used ironically to describe the policy of inaction). But subjects who complained about their situation, or who continued to express views unacceptable to the authorities, were given psychotropic drugs. Patients referred to this as 'punishment by treatment'. One doctor told a patient that if his father continued to write inconvenient letters of protest about his son's treatment, then 'We will make a schizophrenic out of him too.' Koryagin also found that several of the subjects had been detained in hospital on the direct orders of the KGB long after their release had been recommended by their doctors, and instances of this dreadful abuse were quoted with times, places and names.

Koryagin quoted four cases in which subjects were considered fit for military service after being compulsorily hospitalized as dangerous psychopaths and schizophrenics. Ultimately, despite the fact that they had been diagnosed as 'socially dangerous', all the subjects were discharged from hospital without an escort. They were, however, usually given a warning: 'Don't do it again.' Koryagin comments, ironically, 'The patient is dangerous on admission but not dangerous when discharged despite the fact that nothing has changed.'

Koryagin was arrested in February 1981. He had anticipated this and had sent a declaration to the West which stated, *inter alia*:

> I have not committed any criminal act, my arrest will be revenge for my participation as a consultant to the Working Commission. The diagnosis of psychiatric illness is my professional duty as a doctor and can only be criticized by my professional colleagues and not by the KGB and the courts. The result of my trial is a foregone conclusion and I refuse to play any part in it.

The trial began in Kharkov on 3 June 1981.* Koryagin was charged with 'anti-Soviet agitation and propaganda'. Despite the

* A full transcript of the trial has been published by Amnesty International and by IAPUP.

cruel treatment he had to endure in the pre-trial period of interrogation and the great pressure he was subjected to by the prosecution at the trial itself, he remained calm and defiant. When allowed to make a statement in open court he spoke as follows:

> When I began to work for the Commission I became convinced that people in our country who are mentally healthy, are placed in special hospitals because they are dissenters; they may be kept there for years and are compulsorily treated with drugs. My investigation does not constitute an act of justice but a means of suppressing me for my views. I know the sentence will be harsh and that long years of imprisonment, humiliation and mockery await me. But I will not accept the situation that exists in my country where mentally healthy people are imprisoned in mental hospitals for daring to think independently.

The sentence was indeed harsh. Koryagin was sent to a strict regime camp for a period of seven years, to be followed by five years of exile. In January 1986, his sentence was arbitrarily extended for two more years by the camp authorities because of some infringement of the rules. The ability of the camp directorate to increase prisoners' sentences for disciplinary or other reasons is a direct reversion to one of the worst abuses of the Stalin period.

The heroism of Anatoly Koryagin and his dedication to the ethics of his profession are beyond praise. Undaunted by the appalling conditions of the Perm labour camp where he was first sent, he smuggled an open letter to the West which was distributed in the second IAPUP *Bulletin* in October 1981. In it he stated that even after the condemnation of political psychiatry in the USSR at the Honolulu meeting, 'the stain on its white coat' had continued to spread. 'Thousands of dissenters have been sent to psychiatric prisons, many of them are people whose names mean little to anyone.' (Following the international outcry against the abuse of psychiatry in the USSR, the authorities seem to have taken the rather obvious step of reducing the practice in the major cities, where people had some access to the international media, while stepping it up in the remote areas where no such protection could be obtained. This makes a statistical analysis of the problem impossible. Koryagin alerted the West to the fact that the suppression of dissent in the provinces was going on unabated.) Bravely, he called on the WPA to consider whether it should permit the USSR to remain a member while this perversion of medicine was continuing and implored the medical profession not to give up the struggle 'against torturers armed with drugs'.

Constant harassment and frequent confinement in punishment cells failed to break Koryagin's spirit. He did not recant and he kept up a constant battle with the authorities in an attempt to help his fellow inmates with their many medical problems and to maintain their morale. As result, in July 1982, he was sent to the Chistopol Prison, considered one of the harshest in the USSR and the destination of many other intractable cases. The treatment he received in Chistopol brought him close to death. He went on frequent hunger strikes, his only weapon, losing much weight and becoming so fluid-laden due to malnutrition that when his children were finally allowed to visit him they were unable to recognize him.

Meanwhile, protests and appeals that Koryagin should be permitted to emigrate were reaching the highest authorities in the USSR from many countries. In December 1982 I succeeded in getting every member of the executive committee of the Royal College of Psychiatrists to sign a telegram addressed to Mr Yuri Andropov (then Secretary General of the Communist Party) which requested that Koryagin be permitted to resume his practice as a psychiatrist. Another petition signed by virtually every leading psychiatrist in the UK was also sent and similar appeals were made from German, French, Swiss and Dutch psychiatrists and also by many political leaders. All to no avail. It seemed that the KGB were determined to extract a retraction of all his allegations from Koryagin which it could use as a trump card in the campaign which was clearly looming to have the AUSNP expelled from the WPA. But Koryagin was unbreakable.

Koryagin managed to smuggle out a description of the prison conditions he had to endure, including the conditions in the punishment cells to which he was frequently confined. Peter Reddaway received this document and it was published in the *Observer* on 23 January 1983. Anyone reading it could have been forgiven for believing it to have been fabricated by some anti-communist *provocateur*. The conditions described were in no way different to those which prevailed at Belsen and Auschwitz except, of course, for the gas chambers.

Meanwhile, in recognition of his unique contribution to medical ethics, Koryagin had been made an honorary member of nine major psychiatric bodies in the western world, including the WPA. In May 1983, he was awarded the Scientific Freedom and Responsibility Award of the American Association for the Advancement of Science and in December 1985 he was awarded a special prize in Oslo which was, in effect, a token Nobel Prize. I was invited to receive it on Koryagin's behalf which I did. As this award was partly in response to the protest at the actual award of the Nobel Peace Prize to the organization International Physicians for the Prevention of Nuclear War, further mention of this episode will be made later (see page 148).

Meanwhile, a large committee in Holland, which includes 26 members of the Dutch parliament, with a minister and a vice-minister among their number, has nominated Koryagin for the Nobel Peace Prize for 1987 and several former Nobel Prize winners and leading figures in law, history, philosophy and political science have added their support to the nomination.

In October 1986, Koryagin again managed to smuggle a summary of his treatment to date to the West. It was published by the *New York Times*. He stated that he had suffered a total of three years' solitary confinement, had been intermittently on hunger strike for two years, and had spent six months in punishment cells. 'I am waging my struggle for the rights of political prisoners, for their human dignity, for their lives and health, and against the threat of punishment and provocation. Let everyone know that I am standing firm and that I bow to those who are helping me.'

Apparently the prison director told him, 'Your international prizes are a payment for anti-Soviet activity. You should refuse them. (I just laughed at him.)' The director continued: 'You are going to drop dead here. You are not going to have any canteen privileges or visits from your family. You have caused so much harm to the Soviet government it would have been better if you had shot ten people.'

Of his view of the world situation, Koryagin wrote – 'I have three slogans: peace and humanism are inseparable; there should be a striving for peace in the name of humanism and not politics;

only a society with a humane face and laws has the moral right to speak about peace for mankind.'

Koryagin is more than a hero. He is a symbol of the indomitable human spirit. By his actions alone he has proved to the hilt that the accusations made against official Soviet psychiatry are justified, that the abuses persist and that the regime will go to inordinate lengths to protect itself against any attack, especially when ethical issues are involved. But in the end, right will prevail over manifest wrong. This is a law of history from which neither the Soviet Union nor any other country is immune.*

* On 31 January 1987, it was announced that Koryagin was to be transferred to the prison at Kaluga and that permission would be given for him and his family to leave the Soviet Union. He arrived in Zurich on 24 April 1987 and immediately denounced the continued practice of political psychiatry in the USSR. 'Not a single dissident who was confined to a psychiatric hospital has been released,' he said. 'The so-called Gorbachev reconstruction has not touched them at all.'

CHAPTER 22

SHOOT-OUT IN VIENNA

From our point of view at least, the Seventh Congress of the WPA
in Vienna in May 1983 was an anti-climax. We had gathered our
ammunition and prepared ourselves for a shoot-out only to find
that the AUSNP had decided to stay at home – minding the Gulag,
as one wag put it. But it was not entirely a one-sided affair, for
the Soviets did have a few allies from the satellite countries and
the Third World who did their utmost to prevent the passing of
any motion critical of the AUSNP. Indeed, there was considerable
support for the idea that the AUSNP should be invited to reconsider
its resignation.

Moreover there were serious misgivings about the course of
events within the leadership of the WPA itself. Was it appropriate
for a purely scientific body to be concerning itself with ethical
issues? Would not the publicity arising out of the dispute create a
bad image for psychiatry in general? Might not the public conclude
that what was being alleged against the USSR was in fact a
widespread practice in other countries, including their own?
Psychiatrists are, whether they like it or not, part of the social
establishment of their countries, part of the system which upholds
the dominant mode in a society. To attack their role in any one
country might be to tamper, dangerously and unnecessarily, with
the status quo. Much of this was unspoken, but even as a non-
psychiatric witness, an outsider, I was well aware that many of the
participants were thinking along these lines.

Another, and I think stronger, argument against the expulsion
tactic was the view that important reforms may take a long time
to implement. The Soviet Union is a changing society, like every
other, but it changes more slowly than most. Should it not be
given more time, rather than being pushed in a direction which
could well prove counter-productive? After all, the United
Nations Human Rights Commission was already undertaking a

study of the psychiatric abuse issue and it was surely the appropriate body to deal with the matter.

When it came to the crunch the line-up was as follows: the Czech and Bulgarian societies resigned in support of the AUSNP; the Hungarians and East Germans expressed their support for the AUSNP but did not resign; the Cubans resigned with strong expressions of disgust at the political machinations of the US which, they claimed, underlay the whole issue. The Poles did not attend, probably due to lack of finance, but it is likely that, had they done so, they would have been forced to give at least token support to the Russians. But a Polish psychiatrist who did manage to get to the conference told me in private conversation that the Polish profession deplored the behaviour of the Russians and fully supported the stand taken against it.*

After a very confused debate, the General Assembly of the WPA carried an *ad hoc* motion proposed by Professor Rawnsley of the Royal College which said that the WPA would welcome the return of the AUSNP to membership, but only if first provided with real evidence of the amelioration of the political abuse of psychiatry in the USSR. The majority in favour of this motion was an overwhelming one: 174 for, 18 against, 27 abstentions. The size of the majority was to no small degree a tribute to the conciliatory tone of the resolution – one more tribute to the British talent for tact and diplomacy.

Four years after the AUSNP resigned from the WPA under circumstances which amounted to a tacit plea of 'guilty' to the charge of using psychiatry as a weapon against political dissent, the question must be faced: has there been an outcome? and if so, what is it?

No one seems to be able to provide a clear answer to this or, for that matter, to many other questions concerning Soviet policy towards dissidents. Anyone familiar with the course of Soviet affairs knows that nothing short of a catastrophe like Chernobyl is likely to elicit a speedy reaction from the bureaucracy. The Soviet Union will rarely, if ever, respond in a way which might suggest

---

* On later visits to Czechoslovakia and Hungary I was told by psychiatrists there that the political abuse of psychiatry in their countries was quite rare, though not unknown, and that they fully supported the strong stand that the WPA had taken.

that it is yielding to pressure. Moreover, many of the policy-makers have their own position in the scheme of things to consider. It may be recognized that reforms are needed, but this does not mean that they would be implemented if they would result in a loss of status or privilege for those responsible. And even if reforms were taking place, we might not be aware of them; since 1983, and even before, it has become increasingly difficult and dangerous for Soviet citizens to impart information to outsiders. It is indeed a criminal offence to reveal to a non-Soviet citizen information which is either work-related or in any way connected to the security of the state.

The officials who were most closely implicated in the abuse of psychiatry – Morozov, Vartanian and Snezhnevsky – are still in office, but are they still in power? No one really knows. There is some oblique evidence which suggests that the abuse of psychiatry is diminishing: some victims such as Baranov, Grivnina and Davydov have been released and the few prominent dissidents who still remain at large and thus have the opportunity to commit 'offences' are not going to psychiatric hospitals but to camps. It does, however, seem likely that psychiatric abuse is still fairly common in the remoter areas of the country.

Viktor Davydov testified to the Fifth International Sakharov Hearing in London, in April 1985, that while he was still in a psychiatric hospital, after the Vienna meeting, the hospital authorities were ordered to release as many inmates as they could. This was apparently done in an attempt to reduce the number of sane victims of psychiatric abuse and could have been a response to the criticism to which the Soviets had been exposed. There is also some evidence that those dissidents who are still being sent to psychiatric hospitals are not being held for long periods; they are sent for short, sharp sessions mainly to frighten them. A number of members of the Moscow Trust Group have been subjected to this 'therapy'. It is accompanied by an explicit warning – 'Carry on with your nonsense and you will finish up in here for a long time.'

CHAPTER 23

THE KGB'S NOBEL PEACE PRIZE

On 13 October 1985 it was announced in Oslo that the Nobel Peace Prize for 1985 had been awarded to an organization of doctors called International Physicians for the Prevention of Nuclear War (IPPNW).

It is certainly fair to say that in the troubled world of the 1970s and 80s the task of selecting an individual, or organization, who is generally agreed to be worthy of this unique award has become far from easy. Controversial awards such as those made to Henry Kissinger and Le Duc To (who declined it) and Menachem Begin and Anwar Sadat, have resulted in the whole business becoming increasingly politicized. Moreover, although Nobel's will stipulates that the prize should go to the person who has done most to promote harmony between nations, especially by reducing armies and organizing peace-promoting congresses, the scope of the nominations has gradually been widened to include those involved in humanitarian as well as peace-promoting activity.

In 1985 the selection committee had been confronted with 98 other nominations which included Bob Geldof, Simon Wiesenthal, Winnie Mandela and Elie Wiesel.* Despite the claims of these other contenders, the decision to award the prize to IPPNW, apparently in recognition of the organization's work in promoting the need for nuclear disarmament, seemed, on the face of it, to be highly appropriate. But it soon became apparent that although IPPNW proclaimed the most worthy of aims, it was an organization which had, to say the least, a doubtful *provenance*.

Ostensibly it was just a large (and very influential) group of doctors from 41 nations united in a single purpose – the prevention of a nuclear war which they graphically and accurately described

---

* Awarded the prize with worldwide acclamation in 1986.

as 'the final epidemic'. Their message was simple and clear: a nuclear war would obliterate human life from the face of the earth; it could not be survived; there was no means of defence against it; no political or other consideration could justify it; a nuclear war must never be allowed to happen.

The organization had been set up in Geneva in December 1980. The founders were, effectively, Dr Bernard Lown, a Boston cardiologist of great eminence and a Professor at the Harvard School of Public Health, and Professor Yevgeny Chazov, a long standing friend and colleague of Lown's, who was the Director of the USSR Cardiological Institute. Chazov was also a trusted member of the highest organs of the Soviet state. He is a member of the Central Committee and has been personally responsible for supervising the medical care of three Soviet leaders – Brezhnev, Andropov and Chernenko. The directors of IPPNW were of course helped by a number of assistants, but to all intents and purposes, IPPNW *was* Lown and Chazov who were permanent co-chairmen of the organization. The declared aims of IPPNW included the dissemination throughout the world of information concerning the consequences of nuclear war. But in advocating the steps that should be taken to prevent nuclear war IPPNW declared that it would not take a position on the specific policies of any government – in other words, it was to be at all times neutral on political issues. It was, in effect, a single-issue pressure group with a single purpose – the prevention of nuclear war.

The membership was to be open to all doctors and IPPNW claimed a membership of 145,000 including 60,000 from the USSR. The Governing Council was to consist of a representative from every constitutent national member, while the executive committee was to be drawn from a wide geographical area; in 1985 its members were from Argentina, Australia, Hungary, Sweden, the US, and West Germany. So far, so good.

My own suspicions about the *bona fides* of IPPNW were aroused by several factors. I had known Bernard Lown since the early 1950s when I began my postgraduate training as a cardiologist. I had visited him in Boston and studied the experiments which eventually led to the development of the defibrillator – an instrument for restoring normal heart rhythm after it has become disordered, as occurs, for example, in the case of a heart attack. The defibrillator is one of the great advances in modern medical science; it has enabled many lives to be saved and Bernard Lown should have been awarded a Nobel Prize in medicine for his part in the development of it. I had also learned, however, that Bernard held strong views on political subjects and that on almost every issue he tended to be very pro-Soviet and anti-American.

But we had not kept in touch during the intervening years and I had no way of knowing his current political stance. Nevertheless, during the campaign on behalf of Dr Koryagin I wrote him the following letter:

April 21, 1982

Dear Bernard,

Many doctors (including myself) will applaud your achievements in mobilizing medical opinion against nuclear armaments. But many will also feel, as I do, that more effort is needed towards building trust [between the superpowers] and less to emphasizing the horrors of nuclear war. With your long record of openly expressed hostility to militarism, especially in the USA, and your access to the Soviet leadership, you are in a unique position to bring home to the latter, that nothing impedes the process of disarmament so much as the widespread fear of the tyrannical nature of Soviet power. The message which Prof. Chazov brought to your congress [held by IPPNW at Cambridge] from Mr Andropov, in which he declared, 'he had always supported and would continue to support humane activities of physicians protecting the life and health of all people on earth', would carry more conviction if it were not for the fact that it is the same Mr Andropov who is the architect of the repression which has sent every free thinker in the Soviet Union who dared express himself to jail, prison camp, psychiatric hospital or exile with increasing frequency since 1977. This is the man who refuses to allow Andrei Sakharov, or his wife, to receive treatment in the only hospital with appropriate facilities manned by doctors whom the Sakharovs can trust – the Academy's hospital. It is also Mr Andropov who ignores the pleas of the world's scientists to allow Yuri Orlov to go free and who has ignored the pleas of many hundreds of psychiatrists from all over the world to free Dr Anatoly Koryagin and allow him to resume his work as a psychiatrist.

It is certainly a great achievement that representatives of IPPNW were permitted to address 100 million Soviet television viewers [this figure is now known to be greatly inflated, the broadcast was never advertised and was put out during an off peak period] in an unedited, uncensored and unrehearsed broadcast. Surely it would be an equal achievement if Mr Vladimir Danchev [a Radio Moscow commentator who referred to Soviet troops in Afghanistan as 'invaders'] hadn't finished up in a mental hospital.

Bernard, I mention these matters, not to detract from your achievements but because I believe Sakharov was right when he said, fifteen years ago, that nuclear disarmament could not be achieved and might even be dangerous, while the Soviet Government remained free from all constraint by public opinion.

I received no reply.

On 22 March 1984, I again wrote to Bernard Lown, this time on behalf of Mrs Bonner after receiving copies of her electrocardiograms which showed unequivocal evidence of the heart attacks which she had suffered. I knew from her family that she was severely disabled by angina pectoris and suspected that cardiac surgery of a type not available to ordinary citizens in the USSR would be necessary. I appealed to Lown to use his considerable influence to persuade the Soviet leaders to allow Mrs Bonner to travel to the UK for treatment. I said that such a humanitarian gesture would do much to defuse the present dangerous tension.

Again he did not reply.

In fact, Lown adamantly and consistently refused to become involved in the human rights issue. So resolute was he in this attitude that during an IPPNW meeting in Helsinki in June 1984 he refused to take part in an interview with Mrs Bonner's daughter to discuss her plight – this was at a time when Sakharov had commenced a hunger strike and was believed to be in danger of his life. Lown has also refused to meet any member of the Sakharov family that lives in the same Boston area. Lown took the view that the human rights question was irrelevant to the question of arms control, indeed he regarded it as an impediment and believed that it was being used as a weapon to destabilize the Soviet regime. He refused to accept the contrary view – that to ignore the human dimension of the conflict which underlies the arms race is both unrealistic and self-defeating.

But the aspect of IPPNW which bothered me most was the role of Professor Chazov, its co-founder and permanent co-chairman. To expect a trusted functionary of the *Nomenklatura*, the man who oversaw the health problems of Brezhnev, Andropov and Chernenko, to say nothing of countless other members of the ailing leadership, and who was also a member of the Central Committee of the CPSU, to adopt anything but an officially-approved stance on any major issue was to stretch credulity to the breaking point – indeed, the idea was ridiculous.

As for IPPNW's claim that it had 60,000 Soviet doctors among its membership, that whole idea was laughable. If they existed at all, which was by no means certain, they would have been under orders to enrol. Soviet doctors cannot join international organizations without official approval and instruction. Unofficial peace groups do of course exist in the Soviet Union, the most effective – and the most harassed – being the Moscow Group for Establishing Trust Between East and West (The Moscow Trust Group). But the official attitude towards such organizations is indicated by the fact that at least fifteen members of this Group have finished up in psychiatric hospitals and a number, including one of the founders, Sergei Batovrin, have been exiled. Its principal doctor member, an anaesthetist called Vladimir Brodsky, was sentenced to three years in a labour camp for 'suspected hooliganism'. He has been on hunger strike intermittently since his imprisonment.*

But the factor which really made me suspect that IPPNW might be well and truly under the domination of the KGB (even without its many non-Russian members being aware of the fact, or even the possibility) was the role of Dr Marat Vartanian as the organization's principal spokesman in the US. Vartanian was the deputy director of the Soviet Centre for Mental Health and the Institute of Psychiatry in Moscow and served as second-in-command to Professor Snezhnevsky. More than that, he was the principal spokesman for Soviet psychiatry at all international meetings, including those of the Executive Committee of the WPA of which he was a member. In this capacity, between 1971 and

* He was later released after a worldwide protest.

1977, he was deeply implicated in the question of the abuse of psychiatry for political purposes and defended the AUSNP against accusations on this topic many times. Vartanian was clever, charming, plausible and well-liked in many quarters in the West. But the frequency with which he travelled and the authority with which he spoke made him a suspect figure: no Soviet functionary could exercise so much freedom without having the approval of the KGB – or, more than likely, official status within the KGB.

In September 1985 Vartanian and three other members of IPPNW visited Stanford University for a series of meetings designed to promote their cause. These had been sponsored by a separate body, Physicians for Social Responsibility, which had similar though wider aims and which Bernard Lown had been instrumental in forming some years earlier. It was, in a sense, a predecessor of IPPNW and was formally affiliated to that organization. The IPPNW delegation was very prestigious, being led by Academician Leonid Ilyin, Vice President of the Soviet Academy of Medical Sciences. During a session for questions, Vartanian was asked to comment on the allegations concerning the practice of interning dissidents in psychiatric hospitals in the USSR. He replied as follows: 'I can guarantee as a psychiatrist that no one mentally healthy has ever been institutionalized in a mental hospital in the USSR. I am convinced of that fact.' He went on to say that the allegations of psychiatric abuse against the USSR were part of a politically motivated slander campaign which had compelled the AUSNP to withdraw its membership from the WPA.

What Vartanian did not know was that Vladimir Bukovsky, then a student at Stanford, was in the audience – living experience that the liar was Vartanian himself. Bukovsky later told the audience that Vartanian (who is an experimental psychiatrist rather than a clinical practitioner) had participated in the commission which had declared Plyushch to be insane. 'He really is no better than Dr Mengele,' Bukovsky added. The comment might be rather extreme, but not when it is remembered what Bukovsky had endured at the hands of a system which Vartanian was not merely defending but whose existence he was actually denying.

The organizer for Physicians for Social Responsibility subsequently admitted that they had not had any part in the selection of the Soviet representatives who were chosen by the Soviet authorities; indeed, when asked, Vartanian himself said, 'I didn't choose to come here – I was sent by my government!'

Another person present at this meeting, a Professor of English at Stanford, happened to be a cousin of Alexander Podrabinek. He told of the severe punishment that had been inflicted on Podrabinek after he published the evidence of the widespread abuse of psychiatry for political purposes in the USSR and then concluded: 'I feel humiliated by the decision to allow Vartanian to speak here.' Another member of the audience, Professor Louis Lerman, asked a simple question: 'What is a group like Physicians for Social Responsibility doing inviting a person like Vartanian here to talk about social responsibility?' It was a question which seemed to answer itself.

My first reaction to the announcement of the IPPNW's Nobel Peace Prize (I was of course fully aware of Vartanian's activities and fairly familiar with the real position of Chazov in the Soviet hierarchy) was to write a letter to *The Times* setting out the essential facts, which I assumed (correctly as it turned out) were unknown to the members of the Peace Prize selection committee in Oslo. But as the award of the Peace Prize was now a *fait accompli*, *The Times* took the attitude that a more detailed account of the whole matter might be preferable to a letter and suggested that Peter Reddaway should be asked to cooperate in writing it. I readily agreed.

On Tuesday 3 December our article appeared on the Op-Ed page of *The Times* under the banner headline: WHAT SORT OF PEACE DO THESE MEN WANT? In the text itself we claimed that the award devalued the Nobel Prize and gave our reasons. We explained why we believed that IPPNW had in fact been established as part of a Soviet campaign to thwart the deployment in Europe of American medium-range missiles, a step which had been taken in response to the Soviet deployment of ss-20s. We pointed out that, as a member of the Soviet Central Committee, Chazov shared responsibility for the Russian invasion of Afghanistan and suggested that this hardly seemed a satisfactory qualification for a Nobel Peace Prize winner. But most damning was the fact that in 1973 Chazov, along with nineteen other members of the Soviet Academy of Medical Sciences, had put his name to a vitriolic attack on Andrei Sakharov, the Soviet Union's first and most vehement advocate of nuclear disarmament. This letter had played an important part in a KGB campaign which levelled accusations against Sakharov of such outrageous and transparent falsity that known doves, including the Austrian Chancellor Bruno Kreisky, objected.

The campaign was ultimately called off, but the episode reflected no credit whatsoever on Chazov. To start with, the majority of Academicians had actually refused to take part in it, despite the KGB's threats. And the allegations of disloyalty, treachery and treason which were made against Sakharov were in themselves deplorable. Sakharov is a patriot to his fingertips and one of the Soviet Union's greatest sons. It was he, not Chazov, who first warned that a nuclear war would be an unparalleled disaster for mankind and it was, in part, Sakharov's advocacy which had persuaded Khrushchev to sign the Partial Test Ban Treaty. It speaks volumes that such a man could not be a member of the IPPNW as it was then constituted, and the fact that one of its co-chairman was on the record as attacking him in the strongest and most scurrilous terms must cast doubt on all the organization's claims to political impartiality.

Of course, the reasons why Sakharov had been so bitterly assailed for preaching the cause that Chazov would later take up with the apparent approval of his colleagues on the Central Committee were obvious enough: Sakharov had consistently stated that the question of peace and of human rights was indivisible. The refusal of IPPNW to accept this principle is essentially attributable to the fact that the question of human rights was anathema to its sponsors in the USSR. Indeed, any body of Soviet citizens, such as the Moscow Trust Group, who dared to suggest that human rights might be one of the essential factors in a more peaceful world, soon found themselves severely dealt with.

We also pointed out that, as the head of the medical department responsible to the KGB for security matters, Chazov was implicated in serious breaches of ethics, including the whole system of using psychiatry to suppress criticism. That men such as Sakharov and Koryagin should be denied the support which IPPNW could give was incredible but, regrettably, such was the case. We then went on to give further information concerning Marat Vartanian, including the fact that he had recently stated in a Moscow Radio broadcast that two of the dissidents who had been allowed to emigrate after incarceration in Soviet psychiatric hospitals, Natalya Gorbanevskaya and Alexander Volpin, had required constant psychiatric care, including hospitalization, since arriving in the West. This was a complete lie which Gorbanevskaya personally refuted in a telex she sent to me. In it she described how, after the public condemnation of the abuse of psychiatry in the USSR at Honolulu, Vartanian had circulated a series of clinical reports of victims of such abuse among which were her own records. These had been distorted to paint a quite unreal picture of her condition. She said that when she read the protocols of her case to some French psychiatrists they could not restrain their laughter. One of them commented sarcastically that 'we will have to go to the Soviet Union to learn how to cure schizophrenia.'

We concluded that IPPNW was unworthy of the Nobel Peace Prize and that the award could only have been made because the advisers to the selection committee had simply not carried out a thorough enough investigation into the political background of the organization or the track record of the men who were its directors.

Our article was widely and rapidly disseminated through the Western media especially when, in a rather unguarded interview, I described the award as 'the greatest blunder in the history of the Nobel Peace Prize'. But Reddaway and I were far from alone in holding such opinions. Chancellor Helmut Kohl had protested officially against the award on behalf of the Christian Democratic Party and was supported by the leaders of the Christian Democratic Parties of Italy, Belgium, Greece, Spain, Austria, Switzerland, Luxembourg and the Netherlands. This provoked the chairman of the Nobel committee, Mr Jacob Sverdrup, into making a most clumsy and tactless riposte, the gist of which was that no head of government had ever protested at the award of a Nobel Peace Prize except Hitler, who objected when the prize was awarded to the anti-Nazi pacificist, Carl von Ossietsky.

Mr Sverdrup, however, was obliged to admit that the committee had not been aware of Chazov's role in the campaign against Sakharov when making the award to IPPNW and that on receiving the information, he had felt 'uncomfortable'. He was not alone. The King of Norway was said to be most upset, as were many others in Norway and elsewhere.

* * *

Mr Sverdrup was soon to suffer further discomfiture. On 20 November 1985 I received a telephone call from a Norwegian journalist, Viktor Roddvik, who explained that the indignation among the community in Oslo at the award to IPPNW was now widespread and that an influential committee had been formed to organize an alternative prize. The leader of this committee was Egil Nansen, the grandson of the great explorer, Fritjhof Nansen, himself a Nobel Peace Prize winner. The committee had decided to award their prize to Dr Anatoly Koryagin and I was asked if I would come to Oslo and accept it on his behalf. I immediately accepted.

The prize was to be in the form of a brass candlestick, a simple symbol that had been awarded twice before by the Nansens to Nobel winners – Andrei Sakharov and Lech Walesa. The citation to the award cited Koryagin as a brilliant example to the world of civil courage and unselfish devotion to the cause of human rights in the true spirit of Andrei Sakharov himself – for the committee was conscious of the grave affront that the award of the Peace Prize to IPPNW had offered to Sakharov, whose central idea, the indivisibility of human rights and peace, was being so blatantly ignored. My selection as the recipient of Koryagin's award was due to my dual role as a founding member of IAPUP and Chairman of the Sakharov campaign in the UK.

I arrived in Oslo on 6 December and attended a press conference the following day. This attracted a great deal of attention, especially from the Norwegian TV channel, and I was able to explain that IPPNW's claim to be an entirely non-political body was a sham. The ceremony at which the symbolic candlestick was presented was simple and moving. It was accompanied by a declaration which stated:

> Dr Koryagin, by his defence of medical ethics, has won the admiration of the world. His release would be a humanitarian act of great importance and would strengthen international confidence in Soviet sincerity and their frequently proclaimed willingness to promote peace between nations, peoples and individuals throughout the world.

The furore over the Nobel Peace Prize, which was to be formally presented on 10 December, had now become worldwide, and

Oslo found itself thrust into unaccustomed prominence, despite the arctic weather which prevailed. The drama was heightened when, on 9 December, the eve of the Nobel award ceremony, IPPNW held a press conference which I attended as the representative of IAPUP. The meeting was packed – there were estimated to be 150 journalists present as well as innumerable TV cameras. Prior to the conference, anticipating that he was bound to face many questions as to his reasons for signing the letter attacking Sakharov, Chazov had declared that such questions were irrelevant to the issues with which IPPNW was concerned and that he would refuse to answer them. He did, however, release a press statement alleging that Sakharov had advocated the use of atomic weapons by the USA in Viet-Nam and that he had called on the US to increase its nuclear arsenal. The first allegation was entirely false – it had been made previously by Chazov at the time IPPNW was established and was a classic example of the self-serving 'big lie'. The second allegation was a distortion of Sakharov's views and arose out of his correspondence with Professor Drell in which he did claim that until the US increased its ground-based strategic missiles, the existing preponderance of the USSR in these weapons would prevent meaningful discussion on disarmament. Subsequent events were to prove this view to be right. Sakharov was advocating a negotiating tactic designed to lead to the abolition of nuclear weapons, not an increase in such weapons for their own sake.

As predicted, question after question was addressed to Chazov which dealt in one way or another with the Sakharov case. As Chazov stalled and blustered and refused to answer the questions directly, the tide of frustration in the hall rose almost palpably. There was no doubt that, even to the hard-bitten journalists, Sakharov was a hero and that the members of IPPNW sitting up on the stage in front of them represented a fraud and a threat to the preservation of freedom.

Suddenly there was a commotion at the front of the hall – a journalist had collapsed with a heart attack. It soon became known he was a Soviet journalist and a few of the audience seemed prepared to believe that it was a put-up job to take the heat off Chazov. That idea had little to commend it for the patient's heart had stopped and he was clinically dead. But he could not have chosen a safer place to have a fatal heart attack, for he was in the presence of probably the greatest clinical cardiologist in the area of cardiac resuscitation in the world – Bernard Lown. Fortunately, not only was there a surplus of doctors experienced in cardiac resuscitation in the audience, there was also some emergency equipment in the hotel which was quickly and expertly brought into use. Even more providentially the ambulance which finally arrived was equipped with a cardiac defibrillator and, after two shocks, the patient's heart started to beat. He was taken to a nearby hospital and next day a bulletin announced that he was conscious and expected to make a satisfactory recovery. In many respects I regarded this as IPPNW's greatest victory – they had saved a human life and restored humanity to the centre of the debate where it belonged and from which it should never have been displaced.

After the fiasco of the IPPNW press conference I wrote a note to Bernard Lown in which I said:

> In the many interviews I have now given concerning IPPNW, I have invariably included a reference to your great contribution to humanity through your medical discoveries. But in regard to IPPNW I believe you have lost sight of the human dimension of the problem of the risk of nuclear war – Sakharov symbolizes this factor as does Koryagin. Please try and find the time to talk to me on this topic either in Oslo, London or Boston. (Oslo Wed. 11 AM)

For the third time, I received no reply.

However, I did get a telephone call from Dr Ian Maddocks, the Australian member of IPPNW's council, whom I knew, asking if we could meet. I agreed and he arrived at my hotel next day accompanied by an American doctor who was a former council member. I explained my attitude in greater detail and gave them more information about the Soviet manipulation of IPPNW, which they continued to deny. They did, however, agree that many unsatisfactory matters had been given a public airing and they concluded that a two-track strategy should be continued in the search for disarmament. We should continue to advocate respect for human rights and they would advocate a ban on nuclear weapons. Somewhere along the line these approaches might converge. At least, I felt, this could do no harm.

PART THREE

The Campaign for Andrei Sakharov

CHAPTER 24

THE GRAND STRATEGY EVOLVES

I first became aware of Andrei Sakharov's importance through one of my sporadic encounters at the Poetry Society in late 1974 (I learned more about dissent in the Soviet Union at the Poetry Society than I ever did about poetry). At a poetry workshop one evening I had read two short poems; the first was a tribute to Osip Mandelstam:

> *The people need poetry*
> *that will be their own secret*
> *to keep them awake for ever.*
> *Mandelstam*

> You hid in bed
> from the tyrant
> who killed you
> in the end
> but still you sang
> continually
> in praise of life.
> 'Through the black lashes of your Georgian eyes
> affection flowed on everyone around.'

The second was Akhmatova's response to lines of Solzhenitsyn's – 'And while some danced happy and carefree with songs and music, others shed tears no hand could wipe away.'

> Do not disturb
> our snug and cosy lives
> with glimpses
> of tear stained faces
> strangers, of whom
> we know nothing.
> let us enjoy

the endless days
the eventless nights
which stretch peacefully
to the grave.

The verses did not excite much comment from the group, which consisted very largely of female American Eng. Lit. students – I remember that I had to explain who Mandelstam was – and the chairman rather hurriedly called on the next speaker. He was a flamboyant Oxford student with the appearance and voice of Jeremy Irons who read a long, obscure poem about his reflections while taking a sauna bath. These were both intimate and erotic and aroused much comment from the audience – entirely favourable as I recall, although a lot of the poem dealt with a description of sweat dripping off his companion's chin.

My efforts had not been entirely wasted, however, for the next day I received in the post a copy of Andrei Sakharov's essay, *Progress, Co-existence and Intellectual Freedom*, from one of my friends who in fact had liked my Mandelstam poem and thought I would be interested in the Sakharov book. I was indeed very interested.

In the book Sakharov set out the two theses which are basic to all his thinking: first, that the division of mankind threatens us all with destruction and, second, that intellectual freedom is essential to the survival of human society. In expanding the latter idea, it was Sakharov the scientist who was speaking, a man who understood that the key to all biological survival (and mankind was not to be considered as set apart from the biological system) was adaptation to change and that without intellectual freedom, adaptation would be hindered if not entirely frustrated. He went on to list the principal dangers confronting mankind: thermonuclear war, mass hunger, destruction of the environment, the stupefying effects of mass culture and the unforeseeable consequences of rapid technological change.

These problems, he argued, could only be dealt with in the context of universal intellectual freedom. He rejected totally the idea that universal communism was the answer to the world's problems for he believed communism to be fatally flawed by its excessive self-righteousness, the inordinate demands which it made of human nature and, above all, by its intolerance of dissent.

Only a stable, rational society with democratic principles and a government responsive to public opinion could cope with the future or be relied upon to keep the peace. He advocated a 'convergence' of the two major systems, each recognizing the best features of the other and adapting them to suit itself. Above all he warned that a nuclear war would be an unmitigated disaster for mankind because it could not be limited or survived. He went on to urge that the idea of nuclear deterrence, which amounted to mutual suicide, should be abandoned as an irrational policy and in its place there should be a serious attempt to address the causes of war itself. This should start with the acceptance of the right to self-determination of all people. Both revolution and counter-revolution should be regarded as forms of aggression and the superpowers must cease to interfere in every local difficulty with a view to de-stabilizing regimes and extending spheres of influence.

Sakharov's condemnation of totalitarianism in all its guises, including Chinese communism (at that time many people in the West were comparing Mao with Jesus Christ), his warnings of the dangers of nuclear war and his insistence that peace could only be guaranteed by governments which allowed freedom of expression to their citizens and were responsive to public opinion, struck me as compelling, indeed, unanswerable.

Like so many other dissidents, Sakharov had initially been drawn into the movement after Khrushchev had been removed from power by reactionary forces afraid of the liberalization which he had initiated (there is some evidence that Khrushchev himself had become afraid that the process was getting out of hand). As Sakharov's concern with Brezhnev's repressive policies grew, he decided to commit his views to paper – a dangerous thing to do. Soon his writings were circulating in the USSR in *samizdat* form and in 1968 his essay appeared in the West where it made a profound impression.

Over the years Sakharov's views have of course changed to some degree, but his basic theses remain unaltered, and as true now as they were when first enunciated.

By 1984 Sakharov's epic struggle to humanize the power of the Soviet state had captured the imagination of the world. He was the acknowledged leader of, and most revered figure in, the democratic movement in the USSR. His worldwide renown as a scientist, the fact that he was the first great Russian scientist who was entirely a product of the Soviet educational system and his pure Russian family background, made it impossible for the regime to label him 'a Zionist dupe of the CIA'. Indeed, his outspoken criticisms created an awesome problem for the Soviet authorities. As the youngest ever member of the Soviet Academy of Sciences (elected at the age of 32) he had enjoyed public recognition, professional esteem and privileges beyond the reach of most Soviet citizens – these included his own car and driver, a nice apartment, a *dacha* and access to special shops and medical facilities and all the other appurtenances of the good life which are heaped upon the successful Soviet *apparatchik*. There was, therefore, no case for attributing his critical attitude towards the regime to envy, bitterness, a sense of failure, attention-seeking and all the other cliché reasons trotted out to explain away most dissident behaviour. Nor could it be seriously suggested that the Soviet Union's most famous atomic scientist was 'schizophrenic'. Sakharov had every professional and material reason to accept the system as it was, for no one had prospered more from it and no scientist could look forward to a more brilliant future within it.

But Sakharov, driven by conscience and his realization, as a scientist, that the Soviet system was fatally flawed – he called it 'a historical dead end' – and a potential source of catastrophic conflict, had rejected this option and had paid a terrible price for doing so.

In early January 1984 Professor Edward Lozansky, Director of the Washington-based Sakharov Institute, came to see me. He explained that the Institute's purpose was to campaign for the protection and the ultimate freedom of Andrei Sakharov and to promulgate the ideas which Sakharov stood for, in particular, the extreme danger which nuclear war posed to the survival of mankind and the indissoluble link between peace, disarmament and a universal respect for basic human rights. Lozansky asked if I would undertake to form a British committee of the Institute. I agreed.

The Sakharov Institute had decided on two immediate initiatives for 1984. One was the organization of a European tour by a distinguished orchestra made up of emigré Soviet musicians who had agreed to donate their services for the purpose; the second was to consist of a series of scientific seminars to be held in the major European centres of atomic research. I agreed to undertake the responsibility for organizing the UK end of this latter project.

The Washington committee which had set up the Institute was a strong one – its President, Professor Sheldon Lee Glashow, a Nobel Laureate, was widely regarded as one of the world's outstanding physicists, and there were no less than 36 Nobel Laureates on the advisory committee. It was not easy to assemble a British group of equal distinction, but the UK committee did succeed in securing the patronage of Mr David Astor, Sir Bernard Braine DL, MP, Sir Anthony Kershaw MC, MP, Mr Victor Hochhauser, Sir Claus Moser KCB, Lord Rawlinson PC, QC and Mr Tom Stoppard. The executive members included Mr Tom Borges as treasurer and Dr Christine Shaw as secretary.

We decided to undertake two further initiatives in addition to those agreed with Lozansky. We planned to approach the leaders of the principal churches in Britain – the Archbishop of Canterbury, Cardinal Hume (the Catholic Archbishop of Westminster), the Moderator of the Free Church Council and the Chief Rabbi – asking them to address a combined petition to the leadership of the USSR on behalf of Sakharov. We also decided to ask the Campaign for Nuclear Disarmament (CND) for a declaration of support.

On 10 February I received a letter from Efrem Yankelevich, Sakharov's step-son-in-law. (He is married to Mrs Bonner's daughter Tatyana; the family were forced by death threats and other pressures to emigrate and now live in the US near Boston. Yankelevich acts as Sakharov's personal representative in the West.) Efrem enclosed a disturbing document from Sakharov in which he described the perilous situation in which he and Mrs Bonner now found themselves and appealed for maximum effort to avert what he feared might be a catastrophe. In making this appeal, which was dated 23 November 1983, Sakharov drew attention to the intensifying campaign of slander that the KGB was mounting against Mrs Bonner which had assumed a blatantly anti-semitic character. (Mrs Bonner's mother is Jewish and her father, an Armenian, was a founder of the Armenian Communist Party. He perished in a purge.)

The official line now was that all Sakharov's critical opinions were due to his wife's poisonous influence and that this, in turn, was attributable to her 'Zionist connections'. In fact, Sakharov and his wife first met at a demonstration against the trial of a group of dissidents in 1970, and were married in 1971. Long before this, as early as 1957, Sakharov had begun to criticize the Soviet system when he campaigned against the enormous atmospheric nuclear tests then being carried out and the severe radioactive pollution they produced. He had also long advocated far-reaching reforms in the educational system, especially a withdrawal of ideological interference and extension of freedom of expression, and had begun to involve himself deeply in the human rights movement before meeting Mrs Bonner.

This made nonsense of the KGB's claims. But their tactics were nevertheless having the desired effect. The general public tended to regard Mrs Bonner as a traitor and she was occasionally subjected to overt abuse and hostility, particularly on the frequent trips to Moscow (where she still had an apartment) which she made in order to maintain a link between Sakharov, who was of course in enforced exile, and the Western media.

The severe strain of all these pressures, and especially the separation from her children and grandchildren, had caused her to have a heart attack of considerable severity in April 1983 and a second in October. She now had disabling *angina pectoris* and some heart failure. The letter went on to detail the increasing harassment to which the couple were being subjected: their telephone had been disconnected, a policeman was stationed permanently outside their apartment, they were followed by agents wherever they went. Although they both needed medical care, doctors were discouraged from visiting them and Mrs Bonner was afraid to go to the Gorky hospital because she felt that, once admitted, she would be disposed of without anyone being able to defend her or to testify that her death was due to anything but natural causes.

Sakharov believed that his wife's only hope of survival was to be allowed to go abroad for the surgical treatment she so clearly needed. She had applied for an exit visa many times but was refused one.

Efrem suggested in his covering letter to me that it would be helpful if an eminent medical authority in the UK could be persuaded to make a fresh approach to the Soviet leadership offering medical treatment to Mrs Bonner. Fortunately I was in a good position to respond to this request because early in my career as a cardiologist I had worked as a registrar under Professor

John Goodwin, head of the cardiac department of the Post-graduate Medical School, Hammersmith and a former president of the World Cardiological Society. I wrote to him on 17 February, seeking his help which he offered immediately. In my letter I had indicated that if he was willing to help Mrs Bonner, he should write not only to Mr Chernenko but also to Professor Chazov, Chernenko's physician and the leading cardiologist in the USSR, and to Dr Bernard Lown, a close colleague of Chazov's as co-founder of the anti-nuclear group International Physicians for the Prevention of Nuclear War (IPPNW) (see Chapter 23). It so happened, as would be expected, that Goodwin knew both Lown and Chazov well, so he wrote to both men, asking them to use their influence to obtain permission for Mrs Bonner to come to London for medical treatment. He received no reply from either. I also wrote to Dr Lown but had no greater success in obtaining an acknowledgement. Meanwhile I had received copies of Mrs Sakharov's electrocardiograms which confirmed the presence of two separate heart attacks (myocardial infarctions).

On 12 April I wrote, as planned, to the four principal church leaders in Britain enclosing the proposed draft of an appeal asking Mr Chernenko to grant exit visas to Academician Sakharov and his wife so that they might accept offers of medical treatment in Britain. The letter read, in part, 'this appeal is being made on purely humanitarian grounds and with the belief that in granting it, the Soviet Union would be making an important gesture leading to a lessening of tension and encouraging the process of *détente* between East and West'. I indicated that if they agreed to endorse this appeal, a request would be made to *The Times* to publish it.

Doctor Howard Williams, Moderator of the Free Churches and the Chief Rabbi, Sir Immanuel Jakobovits, signed it immediately. But both Cardinal Hume and Archbishop Runcie indicated that, concerned though they were with the plight of the Sakharovs, they preferred to write privately to Mr Chernenko (which they did), believing that quiet diplomacy was more likely to succeed (remote though success by any means seemed to be) than public appeals. This issue of the relative advantages of private rather than public appeals, crops up constantly. I can only say that I do not know of any instance where the Soviet Union has ever responded to private diplomacy and I have never succeeded in finding anyone who does.

All attempts to organize a really effective scientific meeting in

Sakharov's honour were also to prove abortive. The first obstacle to present itself was the attitude of the President of the Royal Society, Sir Andrew Huxley. This was a crucial factor because the Royal Society occupies a unique place in the hierarchy of the world's official scientific bodies: it is one of the oldest of such institutions and can number among its members, past and present, an unrivalled list of scientific luminaries. It was for this reason that we felt that it was the appropriate body to sponsor a scientific meeting in honour of an Academician of such scientific eminence as Sakharov.

Unhappily, Sir Andrew did not agree. He had already made clear, in his Anniversary Address as President of the Royal Society in 1982, that he held strong views on the role of the scientist in matters of a political nature. In his speech Huxley addressed the question as to whether, and to what extent, a scientific body should involve itself in 'moral questions' which are not strictly scientific in nature and which, almost invariably, involve many other considerations besides science. These matters concern value judgements and, said Huxley, 'most scientists would agree that their own views on such matters do not deserve more consideration than the views of other educated people, and a body claiming to represent scientific opinion should not express firm opinions on such aspects.'

Huxley defends his attitude against the charge that it is, in effect, pusillanimous by stating that a body which lays claim to an authority which it does not in fact possess, must in the end lose credibility and, as a result, its opinions will carry less weight when it speaks out on matters that are within its sphere of competence.

One matter which Sir Andrew discussed in detail, and which is highly relevant to the Sakharov affair, is the question of what actions, if any, the Royal Society could appropriately take in regard to the harsh treatment often meted out to scientists in other countries, especially the USSR. The Royal Society had previously been asked to terminate scientific exchanges with the Soviet Academy as one means of protest. This the Society had declined to do and Sir Andrew expressed his approval of the decision. He justified this attitude as follows:

These victims of oppression are suffering not for their scientific opinions, but for political acts unrelated to the fact that they are scientists.* The scientific communities in these countries are not responsible [for this persecution] but they would be the sufferers from any non-cooperation. It would of course be a different matter if scientists themselves were involved in the persecution process such as happened in the Lysenko case [and others] in the USSR.

This argument seemed to me to amount to an acceptance of the proposition that the world's political and ethical problems had grown too difficult and too threatening for scientists to be directly involved. I was reminded of Gladstone's famous remark: 'I leave moral problems for the Archbishop. This leaves me free to deal with the real ones.'

My misgivings were in no way allayed after the interview which Sir Andrew gave to myself, Professor John Humphrey FRS (an eminent biologist who was also a founder of the influential anti-nuclear lobby group, Medical Campaign Against Nuclear Weapons) and Professor J. V. Ziman FRS (an eminent physicist who had campaigned for human rights for many years).†

Sir Andrew was courteous but firm. He said that the Sakharov case had an essential political dimension which took it quite out of the realm of the Royal Society's possible direct intervention. Individual Fellows of the Society, he went on, were prepared to take up the case with Soviet colleagues when an opportunity presented (as, indeed, he had done personally with the President of the Soviet Academy of Sciences),‡ but there was no question of the Society taking any official action such as sponsoring a scientific meeting which the Soviets were bound to find provocative (the whole point of the exercise). In any case, Huxley added, he was not convinced that the Russians did not have a strong case when they claimed that Sakharov possessed important state secrets

* This was certainly quite untrue in Sakharov's case. It was through his experiences as a scientist and through scientific analysis of the problems facing the Soviet Union and the world that he had come to his present position.

† Humphrey and Ziman, together with Paul Sieghart, were awarded the Airey Neave prize for their jointly authored book, *Science and Human Rights*.

‡ In 1986 the then President of the Royal Society, Sir George Porter, took up the case of Sakharov's exile with the President of the Soviet Academy of Sciences and, earlier, the Society signed a joint telegram with the French and Swedish academies of science.

which made it impossible for him to be allowed to emigrate and also entitled them to keep him out of the reach of Western journalists.

The fact that Sakharov had been barred from access to secret work in the USSR since 1968 and that he had, in any case, had many opportunities to reveal secrets to journalists and others prior to his banishment to Gorky if he had chosen to do so, which he had not, carried no weight with Sir Andrew. Nor did a letter from Professor Sidney Drell. This was signed by six leading US atomic scientists, including at least two who had been associated with the construction of the atomic bomb (Hans Bethe and Jerome Wiesner), and stated that in the scientist's opinion there could be no justification for keeping Sakharov in exile on the grounds that he possessed vital knowledge, since nuclear science had progressed too far since Sakharov had access to classified material for any of his information to be secret.

Despite the firm policy of the Royal Society, I thought it would be worth approaching other scientific bodies in the hope that they would agree to sponsor the proposed conference. But when I interviewed Professor T. W. B. Kibble, Head of the Department of Theoretical Physics at Imperial College, he did not feel that there was any chance that a major British scientific institution would sponsor a special meeting in honour of Sakharov without the support of the Royal Society; more importantly, although he was supportive and indeed encouraging he did not think that the time available for organizing such a meeting, approximately four months, was adequate. Obviously, a meeting which lacked prestigious contributors would achieve little, if anything, and might even turn out to be a public relations minus for the Sakharov campaign. I therefore accepted an alternative suggestion made by Professor J. M. Charap, Head of the Department of Physics at Queen Mary College, University of London, that he approach the individual members of university physics departments with a request that they sign a letter which we drafted. The letter, which carried approximately 400 signatures including those of most of the important names in British physics (it would have carried even more had time not been such a crucial factor), read as follows:

from The Institute of Physics, 47 Belgrave Square, London SW1.
to President Konstantin Chernenko, The Kremlin, Moscow.

Dear President Chernenko,
We, the undersigned physicists and other members of the academic community in the United Kingdom, have learned with deep concern of the illness of Academician Andrei Sakharov and his wife, Elena Bonner. We appeal to you, on humanitarian grounds, to take executive action to enable them to travel to London to receive medical treatment for which purpose facilities have been made available by a major London teaching hospital.

CHAPTER 25

SAKHAROV ON HUNGER STRIKE

The work of our Committee took on a new urgency after 3 May, when I received a telephone call from Efrem Yankelevich in Boston with the news that Andrei Sakharov had commenced a hunger strike which he intended to maintain to the death unless his wife was allowed to go abroad for medical treatment. It was now known that she had definitely been refused a visa and, even worse, that she was to be charged under Article 190-1 – the infamous catch-all charge of slandering the Soviet State. (No one brought to trial on such a charge had, so far as was known, ever been acquitted.)*

Efrem emphasized the gravity of the situation. Sakharov had gone on hunger strike once before in 1981 and had succeeded in forcing the KGB to allow Liza, his brother-in-law's wife, to join her husband Alexei in the US. It was unlikely that the authorities would allow him two such victories.

It was obvious that we must redouble our efforts to put public pressure on the Soviets and I thought that the most promising possibility would be to enlist the support of the anti-nuclear lobby in the UK, particularly the Campaign for Nuclear Disarmament (CND). Nuclear disarmament had become a keynote in Soviet foreign policy, especially since the advent of the Reagan administration with its greatly increased programme of re-armament. The maintenance of an extensive nuclear arsenal in addition to their

---

* Mrs Bonner was tried in August and sentenced to five years' internal exile which she was permitted to serve in Gorky with her husband. This was of course an effective way of isolating the Sakharovs from their contacts. But it was not entirely successful. The Soviet Union is so permeated with corruption and cheating that it is always possible to get round official restrictions to some degree, albeit not without danger. The sentence was also the KGB's answer to the growing campaign from abroad to allow the Sakharovs to leave the Soviet Union – 'Of course they could leave at any time – but only when they have served their legally imposed and justly deserved sentences'.

massive conventional forces placed an intolerable strain on the Soviets' backward and inefficient economy and they had invested heavily in encouraging the anti-nuclear campaign in Western Europe. It seemed likely that if CND would take up the Sakharov case, on the grounds that Sakharov was, after all, the first and greatest advocate of nuclear disarmament within the USSR, something positive might be achieved.

I had in fact already approached Monsignor Bruce Kent, the General Secretary, and effectively leader, of CND, on behalf of the Sakharovs on 23 March and had received an extraordinary letter in reply. In rejecting my appeal, Kent wrote: 'CND, in order to preserve the single-issue nature of its campaign, has declined for years to enter into human rights issues East or West or non-aligned, unless they relate directly to rights denied to those working for disarmament in their countries.' This attitude was strikingly similar to that of IPPNW and struck me as very strange. If CND denied that Sakharov had been working for nuclear disarmament, then what did they think he had been doing?

In justifying his position Kent referred to Sakharov's advocacy of further deployment of MX missiles by the US in the famous open letter to Professor Sidney Drell, and his stated opposition to a nuclear freeze.* So far as CND was concerned, Kent explained, these attitudes made it impossible for them to support Sakharov.

In desperation I spoke at length to Sidney Drell about the Sakharov correspondence and he agreed that at the time Sakharov had sincerely believed that deployment of MX missiles was necessary in order to redress the existing imbalance because he felt that, so long as the Soviets enjoyed superiority in land-based intercontinental weapons, they were unlikely to negotiate seriously on nuclear disarmament. The same applied, Drell also agreed, to Sakharov's views on a nuclear freeze. He saw it as a ploy to maintain Soviet superiority which, if accepted, would hinder rather than help disarmament negotiations.† Thus it was Sakharov who was the true advocate of nuclear disarmament; but

---

* Sakharov's letter, which was written in response to Drell's lecture advocating a nuclear freeze, was published in *Foreign Affairs*, June 1983.

† The subsequent history of these negotiations since the Reagan administration increased its nuclear weaponry would seem to confirm this attitude as being substantially correct.

because his policy was contrary to that of the Soviet government he was depicted as a war-monger, a notion to which CND was giving its tacit approval.

In writing a further letter to Bruce Kent on 12 May, I said:

It is clear that this tragic situation [Sakharov's hunger strike] is likely to end in his death. Only a miracle can save this man whom you rightly describe as 'a good person who has suffered greatly'. I appeal to you in desperation to put aside all doctrinal considerations and add your important voice to that of the majority of the world's statesmen and women who have appealed to the Soviet leaders to allow the Sakharovs to go free. Even convicted criminals (which they are not) have the right to access to proper medical care. I urge you to act on the principle, the cornerstone of democratic life, to say nothing of Christian ethics, that no person should be made to suffer for holding views, no matter how misguided they may be, if, as is beyond doubt here, they are held in good faith and conscience.

Bruce Kent's response was to arrange for Bishop Guazelli, the President of *Pax Christi*, to send a letter endorsing the appeal by other religious leaders on behalf of the Sakharovs. But, so far as CND was concerned, he remained silent.

But if the Soviets hoped that everyone in the West would be prepared to remain silent while Sakharov fasted, they were to be disappointed. The extracts from my diary which follow give some idea of the hectic pace of events over the months of May and June 1984 and of the storm of protest and controversy which the case aroused.

5 May

The news of Sakharov's hunger strike has been widely reported and has justifiably aroused great distress and indignation. In an obvious attempt to defuse the situation, the Soviets have released a story to the media that Mrs Bonner was in collusion with the American embassy and was preparing to seek sanctuary in the embassy in Moscow while her husband brought pressure to bear on the government through his hunger strike. 'Only timely measures by the authorities' frustrated this dastardly plot. Friends reported that Mrs Bonner's Moscow apartment was empty [she had sent an advance telegram that she would be in Moscow on 2 May] and under constant police guard. Tass even reported the names of three American diplomats allegedly involved in the plan which was to be the forerunner of a campaign of lies and slanders against the Soviet Union focussed around their alleged mistreatment of Sakharov. The embassy has issued a formal denial of their involvement in any such plan.

With typical restraint, Tass alleged that Mrs Bonner was to become, once she succeeded in getting to the West on the pretext of needing medical attention, 'the leader of the anti-Soviet scum on the payroll of Western intelligence services'. All talk of humanitarian motives was humbug – according to Tass.*

9 May

The Times reports today an account from Irina Kristi, one of the Sakharovs' most trusted friends, who had managed to see Sakharov in Gorky for a few minutes before being hustled away by the police. He had said that he intended to fast to the death unless Elena was allowed to go abroad for medical treatment. Because of her temerity in making this information public, and to prevent further contact with the Western media, Mrs Kristi has been placed under house arrest and her apartment is now under permanent police guard.

10 May

The Soviets have announced that they will not participate in the Olympic Games in Los Angeles because of the many violations of the Olympic ideal by the US and its flagrant abuses of human rights and dignity!! Meanwhile a most disturbing account of Mrs

---

* In a full account of his hunger strike, published in the *Observer* in October 1986, Sakharov described how he had watched as his wife was arrested by the KGB as she was about to board the plane to Moscow on 2 May, after which he had immediately begun his hunger strike. Mrs Bonner had undergone an interrogation during which she was accused of being a CIA agent and was told that she would be charged under article 190-1. A year previously, she had fearlessly described Sakharov's situation in Gorky as analogous to that of the kidnapped Italian leader, Aldo Moro. 'He is in the hands of terrorists who will kill him one day.'

Bonner's physical condition has been given by a close friend, Mrs Natalya Gesse, who says that Mrs Bonner can only walk a few steps without taking nitro-glycerin [against angina] that she is easily made breathless by exertion, and her fingers and lips are constantly blue [due to poor circulation].

18 May

Fear is mounting about the possibility of Sakharov surviving his hunger strike. If he dies, I believe the effect on world opinion will be enormous. He was described, truly, as 'the conscience of mankind' in the citation of his Nobel Peace Prize and his defiance of tyranny and his willingness to die in defence of the concept of legality, makes him a modern Thomas More. I doubt if Chernenko or his henchmen have ever heard of Thomas More, but they cannot be so stupid as to fail to realize what the martyrdom of Andrei Sakharov will mean. If they kill him, they will pay a terrible price which years of sedulous propaganda will not overcome. They will be seen as leading a barbarous regime which will make the world tremble. It is impossible to understand why they cannot see the harm their policy towards the Sakharovs is causing them. It suggests that the present leadership is in the hands of men who are not really rational.

The Portuguese Prime Minister, Mario Soares, has written to the Soviet Prime Minister, Mr Nikolai Tikhonov, asking that the Sakharovs be allowed to go to Moscow for medical treatment or else to go abroad. Thus he joins every other Western leader* in making some sort of protest – Mitterrand, Thatcher and Kohl have already done so, as have the Scandinavian leaders (and their parliaments). The Dutch and Danes have offered the Sakharovs political asylum.

* On 3 May I had received a letter from Sir Geoffrey Howe in response to a letter I had written to him explaining the offer of medical treatment from Professor Goodwin and asking that permission to accept this offer be sought from Mr Gromyko who was due to meet with the British Foreign Secretary in Moscow in July. Sir Geoffrey said in his letter that he had raised the question of the Sakharovs with Mr Gromyko at a meeting in January when he had asked that Mrs Bonner be allowed to go abroad for medical treatment, but Gromyko made no response.

Meanwhile, an influential French editor, Jean Daniel of the leftist weekly magazine, *Le Nouvel Observateur*, claims to have heard from a high Soviet source that the Sakharovs would be allowed to go free if President Mitterrand would take a stand against the deployment of cruise missiles and Pershing 2s in Europe. He suggested that the Soviets had already tried this approach with the Italian Foreign Minister, Giulio Andreotti, while the latter was visiting Moscow recently. Meanwhile Mitterrand is coming under strong pressure from his own Socialist party to cancel a projected visit to Moscow in June unless the Soviets make a reasonable concession to the Sakharovs. Representatives of the ten EEC countries have authorized the French Minister of External Affairs (M. Claude Cheysson) to address a message to Mr Gromyko asking for the Sakharovs to be given their freedom – what a hope!

It seems clear that it is really Gromyko and the Army Minister Ustinov who are now in charge in the Kremlin. Chernenko's role is that of handshaker. With a pair of die-hards like that calling the shots, no wonder Soviet policy is so intransigent. Meanwhile the American ambassador in Moscow has admitted that Sakharov did request that his wife be given political asylum in the embassy while he went on hunger strike but says that this was not agreed.

20 May

The Soviets have pulled out all the stops in a campaign of vilification against Mrs Bonner, who is described in *Izvestia* as 'shallow, resentful, greedy and ready to betray everything and anyone for her own profit. Her basic aim was to force Sakharov into a hunger strike so she could get to the West over his dead body.'

This disgraceful attack provoked the *Guardian* into publishing an anti-Soviet leader – an uncommon event, but one highly indicative of the depth of concern and indignation aroused by the Sakharovs' treatment. It described the *Izvestia* attack on Mrs Bonner as yellow journalism, a phenomenon thought by many to be confined to the capitalist press. It went on: 'The support this ageing couple have given each other, year in and year out, in the face of relentless harassment must be deeply moving to anyone – all politics aside – with an ounce of human compassion.'

This leader encouraged me to write to the *Guardian* [I had done so several times before but never had a letter published]. In my letter [which they published] I gave some facts about Mrs Bonner – her impeccable Communist antecedents, for example. Her father, an Armenian, was a founder of the Armenian Communist Party, and her mother (Ruf Bonner) was an early convert to Bolshevism who devoted her youthful energies to helping overcome illiteracy in rural areas after the revolution. Her father was shot as an enemy of the people during a purge but later rehabilitated by Khrushchev. Elena Bonner served as a nurse in the Second World War and was wounded in the siege of Leningrad and again while serving on a hospital train.*

Meanwhile M. Marchais [leader of the French Communist Party] has stated that, in response to an enquiry, he has been told 'that Sakharov is in a hospital near Gorky and his condition is satisfactory; his wife is in Gorky and is also well'. The French Foreign Minister has replied publicly that no credence can be given to this report and that, in the government's view, the restriction of freedom imposed on the Sakharovs is 'a serious breach of their liberties'. It is not without interest that the French have adopted a very serious attitude on human rights matters (greatly at variance with their reputation for never taking anything except their own self-interest into account) and the Soviet government is obviously trying to mollify them.

[A detailed account of the events of this period has now been published by the *Observer* who have obtained a letter which Sakharov wrote to the President of the Soviet Academy of Sciences on 15 October 1984, in which he explained that most of the alleged slanders for which Mrs Bonner had been sentenced were simply statements which he had made and she had repeated. There were no falsehoods. As for the suggestion that she wanted to get abroad 'over his dead body', had she wished to defect she had had many opportunities to do so when she had been allowed abroad in the past for medical treatment. He observed that he was the only Academician in the Academy's history whose wife had

---

* The utter falsity of the accusation that she was only interested in exploiting Sakharov was amply exposed when, in 1985–6, she was ultimately allowed to go to the US for medical treatment and, on its completion, returned to exile with Sakharov in Gorky.

been made to shoulder the blame for her husband's actions.

Sakharov confirmed that on 7 May he had been seized by KGB agents disguised a doctors in white coats and forcibly taken to the Gorky regional hospital. From 11–27 May he had been subjected to 'the excruciating and humiliating process of force feeding.' His detailed description of the methods used is spine-chilling. If such methods are used on a man whose name is known and revered throughout the world, what happens to the unknown victims? On 11 May, Sakharov suffered an attack which affected his vision and made it difficult for him to walk or write. It was clearly a minor stroke which Sakharov attributed directly to the brutality to which he had been subjected. Sakharov ended his letter with an appeal to the President of the Academy for help and a threat that if this was not forthcoming, he would resign from the Academy – a step which would deprive him of his remaining income but which would bring the Academy into disrepute in the scientific community throughout the world.]

22 May

Thirty prominent Hollywood stars, led by Paul Newman and including Lauren Bacall, Cary Grant, Jack Lemmon, Liv Ullman, and Goldie Hawn, have sent Chernenko a telegram stating, 'Mankind cannot stand idly by and let Andrei Sakharov die.' I thought this a touching gesture – movie stars are too self-centred as a rule to get involved in issues beyond their careers. It is another indication, of which there are now many, of just how widespread is the respect for the Sakharovs and the fear for their safety. Closer to home, the West German Foreign Minister, Hans Dietrich Genscher, has raised the Sakharov issue with Mr Gromyko but apparently received a 'frosty reception'. It seems that the mood in the Kremlin, dictated by Gromyko, is very bleak because of the obvious failure of their efforts to prevent the deployment of cruise and Pershing missiles in Europe.

23 May

I have been in Paris to attend [as an observer] a meeting of the Inter-parliamentary Group [for human rights]. I was very impressed with Madame Weil, a veteran socialist and a great humanist, but rather unimpressed with Ian Mikardo, a veteran

Labour MP, who still clings to outworn dogma as if time had stood still since Lenin's day.

After the meeting I took Tanya and Efrem Yankelevich to tea at the Hotel Meurice in an attempt to cheer them up. Tanya is convinced that Sakharov will not survive this hunger strike and may already be dead. She says that during his hunger strike in 1981, he came close to death after thirteen days and that his resistance would be lower now. [I did not reveal that a few days earlier I had been rung by a reporter from *The Times* seeking information on Sakharov for the obituary which they were preparing.]

24 May

Tanya has had a very moving audience with Pope John Paul II who was, she reported, very sympathetic and fully informed on the Sakharovs' situation. He promised to do all in his power to help. Tanya also had a meeting with the Italian Prime Minister, Signor Craxi, to whom she expressed her fears that Sakharov was already dead.

25 May

In a thought-provoking article in the *International Herald Tribune*, Anthony Lewis claims that the Soviets' intransigence is the direct outcome of Reagan's confrontational policies – his emphasis on rearmament, his rhetorical attacks ('the focus of evil in the modern world') and his open support for Soviet dissidents. All this (says Lewis) has caused the Soviet leadership to close ranks and to conclude that they have nothing to gain by making concessions. Lewis says that the Nixon–Kissinger approach was much more productive – apparently he has forgotten about Afghanistan and the introduction of surrogate Russian military power into Africa. Certainly the state of relations between the USSR and the USA could hardly be worse than it is now. The Geneva arms talks have been broken off, a new and more brutal military campaign has started in Afghanistan, emigration has been virtually halted, the Olympic games boycotted. The Sakharov situation has to be seen in this context.

26 May

Kevin Klose, who I think is one of the best informed of all journalists on the USSR, has written an excellent article in the *Washington Post* which rebuts the views of Anthony Lewis. He believes that the Soviet regime is obsessively afraid of human liberty and the freedom of movement and communication which must inevitably accompany it. The events in Poland, particularly the direct challenge to the authority of the Communist Party, gave the Soviets a great fright. Their response included resuming the jamming of foreign broadcasts in the hope of increasing the isolation and control of the Soviet population, a virtual end to emigration, the ending of direct international telephone communication and a restoration of the control of all outgoing calls via operators (and the KGB). This has been accompanied by the introduction of Draconian laws, reminiscent of the Stalin era, which make it a crime for a Soviet citizen to pass on to an outsider any information concerning his work. Inmates of prisons and camps can have their sentences arbitrarily extended by the prison authorities for such offences as lack of discipline or failure to cooperate in achieving work norms. Added to all this is the fear that any concessions that the Soviets now make will enhance the prospect of Reagan's re-election. Thus the Sakharovs, armed with nothing but their integrity and moral fortitude, must endure the full savagery of a superpower that is totally indifferent to public opinion at home or abroad. The prospect is bleak in the extreme.

28 May

I flew to Paris to attend the concert of the emigré orchestra at Notre Dame along with the Lozanskys and Sheldon Lee Glashow, President of the Sakharov Institute. The church was packed, the music superb and fitting to the magnificent setting.

The leader of the orchestra, Lazar Gosman, I found to be delightful. He is a musician of the greatest ability and led the Leningrad Chamber Orchestra for many years, before emigrating to the US in 1977. He made a number of highly praised recordings with Shostakovich and Benjamin Britten. The orchestra of sixteen musicians included former members of the philharmonic orchestras of Moscow, Leningrad, Odessa and the Bolshoi theatre.

30 May

The Australian Foreign Minister, Bill Hayden, a former police-man and a great humanist, apparently got under Mr Gromyko's skin during an interview in Moscow (according to the *Guardian* and other newspapers) by speaking rather bluntly about the Sakharov case and asking for information concerning his where-abouts and state of health. Gromyko is said to have lost his temper and repeated categorically that the Sakharov case is a purely internal matter and that the Soviet government will not tolerate interference from outside concerning it.

5 June

The time for our concert at the Queen Elizabeth Hall finally arrived. I must confess I was anxious. The orchestra had already performed in about eight major cities in Europe, travelling in a special bus adorned with posters advertising the Sakharov case. Not without reason, they were exhausted and somewhat disgruntled.

In fact, when I went to have breakfast with *maestro* Gosman at the White House Hotel where they were staying, I was confronted with a situation close to mutiny. The problem had been com-pounded by Lozansky's rather imperious manner (he had travelled with the orchestra and was in charge of all arrangements). To make matters worse, the minimum payments that had been promised the players had not always been forthcoming. I was able, to some degree, to overcome the latter problem, using resources which we had accumulated in anticipation of problems of this sort. (Soviet emigrés are notoriously bad at handling money problems, which is not surprising as few have had any experience of personal finance.)

With a little spending money the orchestra took off in better spirits to do some shopping in Oxford Street. They promised to be back in time for the afternoon rehearsal and they were.

But behind our anxiety there was gloom as well because of the fear that Sakharov might already be dead. His step-daughter, Tanya, was convinced of this. The actual arrangements for the concert and the reception which followed it were excellent, thanks to the care taken by the Hochhauser organization. The orchestra played superbly, especially the Shostakovich Sinfonietta. It has been an exhausting and difficult function to arrange but, in the end, well worth the effort.

20 June

I have been in Washington for some days attending to business connected with the psychiatric abuse question mainly. However I did manage to meet up with Efrem and he asked me for an opinion on a plan to offer a reward publicly for information concerning the whereabouts of the Sakharovs and their state of health. It was an indication of the family's desperation that they should even consider such a proposal, which I strongly advised them to abandon. I thought it would not be productive and that the media might regard it as a publicity stunt. In any case, I couldn't see how it could produce more information than was already available through existing channels, both official and unofficial. I was told that anything can be obtained from the Soviet Union by bribery – it is simply a question of 'how much'.

21 June

The *Washington Post* carried a news story today, prominently displayed, that the Sakharov family were offering a reward of $10,000 for information leading to direct contact between them and Dr and Mrs Sakharov. This was clearly an act of desperation. I do not like it but I can understand the family's sense of despair. [I never found out if the reward was claimed and I doubt if anyone will ever know.]

22 June

I went with the Yankelevichs to a special showing of the film *Sakharov* at the John F. Kennedy Centre in Washington. I had seen it previously with the Yankelevichs and several Russian emigrés who are portrayed in the film, including both the Litvinov granddaughters and their mother. I thought it a remarkably good film – Jason Robards plays Sakharov with great solemnity and restraint, Glenda Jackson plays Elena Bonner. The supporting cast are very close to the real life characters as I know them and the general handling of the theme is restrained but powerful and, in the end, moving.

23 June

President Mitterrand has stunned the Soviet leaders by breaking with diplomatic protocol during an official banquet held in his honour in Moscow, and referring to the Sakharov problem by name. He explained that he had no wish to interfere in any matter which the Soviets considered their internal business, but that Moscow's contractual obligations under the Helsinki agreement made such matters the legitimate concern of the other signatories to that agreement. His remarks were tape recorded and later played back to journalists.

Mitterrand apparently said that Sakharov was a symbolic figure in the West and that this must be understood by the Soviets. Their treatment of him was of the greatest importance outside their country and was being watched with care and anxiety. He attempted to soften the blow by saying that his frankness arose from his feelings of respect for his hosts. Chernenko's response to the charge of Soviet violation of its human rights obligations was the standard one – 'with our record on unemployment [i.e. we do not have any] and free education and health care for all, those who attack our human rights record only provoke an ironic smile'. Reporting these events, the *New York Times* claims that M. Marchais has warned Chernenko that if anything dire happens to the Sakharovs, the French Communist Party will sever all links with the CPSU. In fact, similar concern within the French socialist party is so great that Mitterrand came close to having to cancel his visit to Moscow over the Sakharov affair.

CHAPTER 26

THE FIFTH INTERNATIONAL SAKHAROV HEARING

On 10 November 1984, Efrem Yankelevich came to see me in order to settle a question we had been discussing by telephone and letter for some months – the idea of holding the Fifth International Sakharov Hearing in London in April of the following year.

The Sakharov Hearings were already well-established as an important event in the human rights calendar. There had been four so far: the first in Copenhagen in 1975, the second in Rome in 1977, the third in Washington in 1979, and the fourth in Lisbon in 1983. They are not about Sakharov but are held in his honour and their purpose is to foster the cause of human rights in general.

I was, however, by no means enthusiastic about the proposal for several reasons. First, the organization of a three-day event involving participants from all over the world who speak many different languages and represent many different, and often conflicting, points of view, is a daunting physical challenge – to say nothing of the cost. I had been warned by friends who had been involved in the organization of earlier Hearings that, perhaps inevitably, they provided a forum in which disparate dissident groups tried to gain media attention for their views, some of which were, to put it mildly, somewhat extreme. But my main worry stemmed from Efrem's determination that the Fifth Hearing, coinciding as it did with the tenth anniversary of the signing of the Helsinki Final Act in August 1975, should take as its main theme Soviet compliance with the human rights provisions of the Helsinki agreements. Once it had been established, as was inevitable, that this had been very defective, Efrem wanted the participants to consider the whole question of the future of the Helsinki process. This, of course, involved the wider question of the future of détente in which the Helsinki Final Act was an important factor.

I knew that there was an influential and growing political lobby in the us, composed largely of former inhabitants of the Eastern ·

European countries and the Baltic states which had either been taken over by the USSR or had come under their control, which saw the Helsinki agreement as a betrayal that, in effect, legitimized the postwar boundaries of Europe. This was not, in fact, so – the Helsinki Final Act spoke only of the inadmissibility of changing European frontiers by force. In any case, only a madman could believe that any significant change in Eastern European boundaries could come about other than through a slow process of evolution and with the agreement of all the parties, and the Helsinki process allowed for this. Unfortunately there has always been a large extremist element in the US which regards the Yalta agreement as a betrayal (a view which totally disregards the military-political realities of the time) and which seems prepared to contemplate an all-out struggle, not stopping short of war with the USSR, as a viable option.

No political party can afford to ignore this element entirely and certainly not the Republican party. Even Eisenhower, the most popular presidential candidate since Lincoln, had to make gestures to this constituency, the existence of which is a potent factor behind the insecurity of the USSR and the continuation of the arms build-up.

It was obvious that the information we already had on the human rights situation in the USSR, especially since the invasion of Afghanistan, would lead inescapably to the conclusion that the Soviets had failed to keep the promises which they made at Helsinki. But even to pose the question, 'What is the future of the Helsinki process?', was to imply the answer, 'Scrap it'. This would be provocative in the extreme to the Soviets (that was, of course, the whole idea) and would run contrary to the policy, as I understood it, of both the US and the UK. I had spoken to Ambassador Max Kampelman who led the United States delegation at the CSCE meeting in Madrid (see Chapter 17) and also to members of the British CSCE team. Not one of them advocated ending the Helsinki process* although they acknowledged that the dialogue to which it gave rise seemed to achieve very little, if anything. But, at least it provided a properly constituted forum at

---

* The term 'process' is used to indicate that the Helsinki Final Act provided for periodic review and change.

which charges could be laid and evidence presented and which attracted considerable media attention. There was nowhere else where this could be done except for the Human Rights Commission of the UN which was so hamstrung by the UN voting system which more or less assured the Eastern bloc a built-in majority under all circumstances, that it had, to all intents and purposes, ceased to be an arena for useful discussion.

I finally agreed to take on the assignment, knowing that if I did not, there would be difficulty in finding someone else to do the job, and feeling that the best way to prevent the proceedings going over the top was to be in charge of the arrangements. I had had assurances from Martin Dewhirst, Peter Reddaway and Michael Scammell that they would serve on the executive so my own inexperience in the complexities of Soviet politics would not be too much of a handicap. Martin Dewhirst's presence was crucial to the whole scheme because of his knowledge of Soviet affairs, his contacts with the emigré world, especially its innumerable factions and publications, and, above all, his experience with previous Hearings.*

We had to act quickly as the time available for planning was very short. But we were lucky from the start. First, Simon Wiesenthal agreed to serve as the Chairman of the Hearings. Not only is he a charismatic figure, he also carries a very great moral authority which stems from his simplicity, sincerity and fearless commitment to humanistic values. I found him a delightful companion. Nothing illustrates his modesty and simplicity so much as his attitude to the problem of security. We had worried about the cost of providing guards for him during the four or five days we wanted him to stay in London. After all, as the chief scourge of unpunished Nazis, he had plenty of enemies. But when I broached the subject he replied that he never travelled with a security guard

---

* Martin Dewhirst is Lecturer in Slavonic Studies at Glasgow University. At the time of the Hearings Peter Reddaway was Senior Lecturer at the London School of Economics. He had an unrivalled experience of Soviet politics and is regarded as the world's leading authority on the subject of the political abuse of psychiatry. He is now secretary of the Kennan Institute, Washington. Michael Scammell had been editor of *Index on Censorship*. At the time of the Hearings he was completing his biography of Solzhenitsyn which was subsequently to be praised as the definitive work on this difficult subject as well as a literary masterpiece.

and did not expect us to provide one. He simply accepted the constant danger as part of the price he had to pay to do his work. Naturally I took the precaution of contacting Scotland Yard, not only about Wiesenthal but also about a number of other visitors, and with the greatest professionalism they took matters in hand and provided round the clock protection in a highly effective manner, but so inconspicuously that none of the subjects knew they were under constant police protection.

Arranging the agenda took many hours of discussion and dispute.* One of the first and most important decisions we made was to reduce the duration of the Hearings from three to two days. My experience of scientific meetings suggested that the longer the proceedings, the more diffuse they become. The attention span of the participants and the media is impaired and an over-long agenda only encourages long-winded and irrelevant disputation. Efrem opposed the proposal, largely for fear that many topics and speakers would have to be eliminated (which was true) and that this would give rise to much recrimination (also true). But the advantages (as I saw it) outweighed the disadvantages. I did not see the point of a talk *fest*. I wanted the Hearings to be primarily a media event and felt that if they failed in that respect, it would not really matter how many speeches were made. They would have little if any impact on events. Fortunately the Executive Committee supported my view.

Efrem gave a brief and effective opening address; setting, I thought, a very good example to the speakers who were to follow. (Russians are very rarely brief when given a public opportunity to air their views. On the contrary, they always seem to be convinced that what they have to say is epoch-making and that, irrespective of prior agreement, they must be given unlimited time to say it.) Efrem emphasized Sakharov's commitment to the concept of détente, but only to a détente which implied a progressive democratization of the Soviet Union. Détente based simply on fear of Soviet expansionism without any attempt to alter fundamental Soviet attitudes to human rights, would not, in Sakharov's view, bring the world freedom from the fear of war – quite the contrary. The human rights question was vital in any discussion of

---

* Only brief details of the agenda will be given here as the *Proceedings* were published in full by André Deutsch in 1986.

the future of détente, for peace and human rights were indivisible.

The first paper was to be the keynote contribution – a learned account of the legal status of human rights activism. The importance of this topic cannot be over-emphasized. Whenever the Soviet Union's human rights record is brought up, in whatever forum, the Soviets' stock reply is that this is a purely internal matter and that no outside body has any business to discuss it, and they reiterate with depressing regularity that a concern for the human rights of Soviet citizens is 'an illegitimate interference in the internal affairs of a sovereign state'. To address this issue we were lucky to obtain the services of Paul Sieghart, chairman of the British section of the International Commission of Jurists and an acknowledged authority on International Law.*

Sieghart started by dismissing as arrant nonsense the notion that only capitalists believe that the individual person has inalienable human rights. Even the socialist countries, by their acceptance of the Universal Declaration of Human Rights of the UN and the International Covenant on Civil and Political Rights, are legally committed to the concept that the individual has certain inalienable rights. These binding international laws, Sieghart explained, have the effect of converting the individual from 'an object of international compassion into a subject of international right'. The present position is that the rights of individuals everywhere have been codified and that any abrogation of these rights is a legitimate concern of the international community. The fact that there is no machinery for enforcing compliance with international laws does not, in any way, make them less binding in the moral or political sense although clearly it poses an insuperable problem in practice.

Rejecting the Marxist thesis that laws only exist to protect the interests of the ruling classes and that the real determinants of human progress derive from politics and power, Sieghart spoke forcefully. 'Freedom cannot exist except under the rule of law; the law is there to protect the weak against the strong, the poor from the rich, the stupid from the clever, and the citizen from the state.' Nothing honours Sakharov more than an unremitting quest

---

* His book, *The International Law of Human Rights*, Oxford University Press, 1983, has been described by Lord Gardiner as 'the last word on the subject for years to come'.

to bring about those changes which will confer on the citizens of the Soviet Union the protection of the law which they do not at present possess and without which they cannot be free from tyranny or the world safe from war.

Sieghart was followed by a succession of speakers who gave an authoritative account of the changes in Soviet criminal and administrative laws (all of them regressive) which had taken place since August 1975 when, in putting its name to the Helsinki Final Act, the Soviet government had promised to increase the human rights of its people. Even the monitoring groups which citizens had set up to report on compliance, in accordance with the Act, had been disbanded – virtually all their members were imprisoned, exiled or committed to psychiatric hospitals. The restrictions on religious activity were well documented by Michael Bourdeaux; the virtual halting of emigration was quantified; and such blatant violations as the resumption of radio jamming, postal censorship and the interference with the freedom of journalists also described in detail. David Satter, who had been a Moscow correspondent for the *Financial Times* for several years, gave a splendid and candid insight into the way the Soviet authorities manipulated representatives of the Western media and explained how easy it was for them to plant incriminating information on a journalist whom they wished to compromise [as later happened in the case of Nick Daniloff]. Representatives of various national groups, including the Crimean Tartars, the Ukrainians, and refugees from the Baltic states, gave personal accounts of the severe repression of all nationalistic activity in the USSR. The story of the persecution of the Crimean Tartars, as related by Aishe Seitmuratova, was especially moving. Although, for reasons of time, the resurgence of official anti-semitism was not considered as a separate issue, Simon Wiesenthal gave 26 individual media briefings during which he provided ample evidence of the blatantly anti-semitic campaign which was then under way, with official blessing, in the USSR. The subject of official anti-semitism naturally came up frequently in connection with other topics such as emigration policy and the nationalities question.

Much of the important evidence concerning human rights abuses in the USSR came from former victims who had recently emigrated. These included Viktor Davydov who had been an important dissident since his student days in Kuibyshev when he had taped readings from Solzhenitsyn's *Gulag Archipelago* to distribute among his friends. Davydov's dissident activities, in which he had persisted despite warnings from the KGB, first led to his committal to a psychiatric hospital in 1977 when he was declared to be schizophrenic. In 1979 he was carefully examined by Dr Voloshanovich on behalf of 'The Commission' (see Chapter 15) whose report concluded that he had found no evidence of mental abnormality. In 1980, after an examination at the Serbsky Institute, Davydov was once again committed to a psychiatric hospital where he remained until 1983 and was compulsorily treated with large doses of psychotropic drugs. He was allowed to emigrate in early 1985.

Davydov described the impact of his admission to the psychiatric hospital in Kazan thus:

In my first days in the hospital I suffered a gigantic shock – a shock which destroyed any ideas I had about humanity, justice, goodness and man's noble destiny. I watched sane people go insane and become mute animals. THIS WAS NOT AN OBSERVATION BY AN OUTSIDER BUT MY OWN PERSONAL EXPERIENCE.*

His detailed description of his treatment and its effect was most disturbing – it could only be described as torture by drugs. Later in his confinement his conditions had improved considerably and this he attributed to his adoption as a prisoner of conscience by a group in West Germany. This was one more indication among many that the intervention of groups like Amnesty often does help prisoners in the USSR.

Davydov mentioned that a circular had been sent to his hospital in May 1983, offering all the political prisoners their freedom if they were prepared to sign a guarantee that they would refrain from further political activity. Another circular from the Serbsky Institute instructed the staff to declare as many inmates sane as possible. This was probably a response to the outcry abroad over the political abuse of psychiatry which had led to the Soviet

---

* Davydov has been examined by a commission of psychiatrists in the US who found no evidence whatsoever of mental illness.

withdrawal from the World Psychiatric Association. It seemed as if our long campaign was not without some effect after all.

Equally moving and effective testimony was given by Georgy Davydov, a geological engineer, concerning the inhuman conditions in prison camps. His involvement in dissident activity had resulted in his confinement to Vladimir Prison and to various camps in 1972. He served five years and emigrated in 1980. His description of the camp regime – the starvation rations, the permanent hunger and cold of the inmates, the strict control over correspondence, the arbitrary punishments for infringements of the rules, the constant threat of physical violence and the ever present danger that the prisoner's sentence would be arbitrarily extended – made a deep impression on the audience. Again this was first-hand evidence. What emerged, inescapably, was a picture of a totalitarian regime prepared to use the utmost brutality to preserve its power.

The most contentious and important part of the Hearings took place on the second day when the question of the future of the Helsinki process was considered. The opening speaker, Peter Reddaway, started the ball rolling with a brief but authoritative account of the effect of Western pressure on Soviet internal policies. This is a topic which has caused dispute and confusion ever since the Second World War when the West began to grapple with the ambitions of the Soviet super-state. One school of thought argues that Soviet internal policies were governed purely by Marxist dogma and the perceptions of its ruling élite, and that no external pressures could have any effect – were likely indeed to be counter-productive. Another school holds that external pressure has had some effect – though never a decisive one, because it is important to the Soviet leaders that they never appear to be giving way to external forces and that they never lose face. This makes the diplomatic approach difficult and it is often almost impossible to establish the relationship between cause and effect.

The problem of assessing the effect of any course of action by the West on the Soviet leadership is complicated by the lack of any feed-back from the media. There is no way in which the Soviet public can express its views and no debate within the bureaucracy ever becomes public. Reddaway has become expert in reading the internal evidence of what is really happening in the USSR. He believes that Western pressures can have an effect on policy, though it is never decisive and is always subject to reversal. Despite this, he argues, the West has more leverage on the Soviet Union than it realizes and should use its power with greater resolution and coordination.

In particular this applies to economic power and the control of technology. In both these areas the Soviet Union is very dependent on Western help, and is growing increasingly so as it falls further and further behind in the technology race. The Soviet Union has an intense urge to expand its power politically, geographically and militarily, and this it can only achieve by increasing its economic power. It is also acutely sensitive to the question of prestige. It is well aware that its image as a repressive, totalitarian state is less than attractive to many people who might, in other respects, be favourably disposed towards it. It is thus depriving itself of an important source of support by following policies which in themselves have a doubtful validity – would it matter if there were ten more Solzhenitsyns? Is the criticism of a Sakharov so decisive that he has to be treated without a scrap of legality to say nothing of humanity? Reddaway emphasizes that the Soviet leadership is still hard-headed in its calculations – it applies the same Leninist principles now as it did in Lenin's day: where does the power lie? what is the constellation of forces? These are the decisive considerations and friendship, treaty obligations and so on count for little when set against them.*

Reddaway suggested that the deterioration in the human rights situation in the USSR which had proceeded progressively since 1979, seemed to be bound up with a power struggle within the Brezhnev regime. He and his successors continued to follow a repressive policy, especially after the invasion of Afghanistan, as they felt that they had nothing further to lose by way of international prestige.

Reddaway urged that, in every international forum in which the USSR was represented, the West should cease to take the defeatist attitude that 'criticism achieves nothing' and should go all out to

---

* It is interesting, and disturbing, to read the number of references to the infallibility of Lenin and Leninism in Gorbachev's speech to the 27th Communist Party Congress. If he has modernized his attitudes, he certainly dare not depart in public from slavish adherence to the source of official dogma, and almost certainly he does not deviate in any significant sense in private either.

demand reforms as it had done, with outstanding success, on the issue of psychiatric abuse. Finally he urged that the West should threaten to break off the Helsinki process if reforms were not forthcoming. He added that there was no likelihood that such a threat would have to be carried out: if it was made with conviction, the Soviets would make concessions to avert the danger.

I must say I was rather uneasy at this overt advocacy of a strategy which I believed to be wrong in both political and practical terms. But Reddaway's credentials were great. He was far from being a 'cold warrior', anxious to challenge the communist superpower on any and every pretext. His views, I knew from long experience of them, were firmly based on evidence and careful reasoning.

Following Reddaway's paper, the same theme was taken up by the Soviet historian and author Michael Voslensky whose book, *Nomenklatura*, had done so much to expose the true nature of the Soviet bureaucracy. He stressed that it is important to the Soviet bureaucracy that it be seen to have observed its international obligations scrupulously. Thus all exposures of the falsity of this claim are significant and are likely, in time, to lead to rectifications. In regard to the view, often expressed in the West, that delicate negotiations on human rights questions are best conducted privately, Voslensky is scathing – secret negotiation may well have an effect but only if it is backed up by vigorous public exposure of the issue. The Soviet official does not respond to appeals to decency, clemency, humanity or any other bourgeois subjectivism. He responds to the 'constellation of forces'.

These two speakers were followed by Mr Elliott Abrams, US Assistant Secretary of State. He gave, in a very authoritative manner, the current State Department view. First, he agreed with Reddaway in attributing the increasing repression which had begun in 1979 primarily to the instability resulting from the prolonged leadership crisis in the USSR. With its economy growing worse by the day and its leaders more incapacitated, the regime felt that it could not tolerate the increasing dissent and the resultant social instability; hence the decision to crack down. Abrams suggested that the arrival of Gorbachev on the scene might result in an amelioration of the human rights situation but it was, of course, too soon to say. The Soviet government had claimed in its discussions with the US that only an improvement in

Soviet-American relations was likely to improve human rights questions in the USSR. The US had responded by stating that the abuse of human rights in the USSR was a barrier to improved relations. The US wanted deeds rather than words and would not reward promises alone.

Abrams then proceeded to give an expert and insightful account of the factors affecting Soviet internal policies. He explained that external events had only a marginal effect. But despite the apparent lack of achievement in the human rights field, the Helsinki process was valuable in that it provided opportunities for every signatory country to raise the issue with the Soviets and their allies. The fact that they did so meant that the human rights issue got coverage in the media when it might otherwise have been ignored. This was very important in the constant struggle for the 'hearts and minds' of the non-aligned people of the world, to say nothing of the effect on people who would in other circumstances be sympathetic to the Soviets. To abandon the Helsinki process because of its apparent failures would, in his view, be a mistake. As he put it, in summing up, 'There may be divisions on arms matters or political questions [among the NATO, neutral and non-aligned nations] but there are no divisions on Sakharov.'

The Foreign Office view was ably presented by John Mac-Gregor, Assistant Head of its Soviet Department. He decried any effort to use a carrot and stick approach with the Soviets on the human rights issue and suggested that this had been a mistake made by the Carter administration. He stressed that all major issues with the USSR were essentially long-term. Nothing of real importance could be expected to eventuate in the short term. A constant reiteration of the human rights question in conjunction with the other outstanding issues, especially arms control, might, in the long run, have the desired effect. Patience and persistence should be the keynotes.

An important contribution was made by Gerald Nagler, Direc-tor of the Helsinki Federation, concerning the meeting of the human rights experts of the CSCE due to take place in Ottawa the following month. He urged that delegates should insist on the release of all imprisoned members of Helsinki groups in the USSR as well as members of Charter 77 and the Committee to Defend the Unjustly Persecuted in Czechoslovakia, the Committee for

Social Defence in Poland, the Turkish Peace Association and all other defenders of human rights including journalists and editors. He also called for the setting up, within the Helsinki framework, of a permanent fact-finding commission which could receive submissions concerning human rights violations from individuals and non-governmental groups. This body should be given the right of access to victims of alleged abuse and the right to make on-site inspections. I thought this suggestion to be a very appropriate one which, if adopted, would give the Helsinki process real authority which it certainly lacked at present.

The Final Resolution of the Panel was delivered on 11 April 1985. It concluded with regret that the evidence showed that there had been a profound deterioration of the human rights situation in the USSR since 1975 and that this was reflected in its laws and practices. There had been a dramatic increase in the persecution of individuals claiming human rights to which they were entitled under international law, a dramatic decrease in emigration, increasing persecution of religious and ethnic minorities, an increase in radio jamming and other interference with international communication and a deterioration in cooperation in the cultural and scientific area. The Panel recognized that human rights violations were not confined to the USSR and deplored them wherever they occurred. It called for the material gathered at the Fifth International Sakharov Hearing to be conveyed to the appropriate bodies of the signatories to the Helsinki Final Act (which it was). It urged the participants at the forthcoming meeting in Ottawa to take appropriate steps to amend 'the deplorable state of Soviet human rights policies'. Finally, the Panel called on the governments of the West to take all steps to secure the restoration of the Sakharovs' freedom, including their rights to emigrate. This resolution was signed by the Chairman of the Panel, Simon Wiesenthal.

That the Hearings passed off without any blood being spilled was probably due more to luck than good management. The account given here is a bare outline. The real business (as with most conferences and international meetings) took place between groups in hotel lobbies, rooms and coffee bars. There was a lot to talk about, a lot to complain about, a lot to dream about.

CHAPTER 27

MRS BONNER'S RESPITE

On 30 October 1985 we heard that Elena Bonner had been told she would be allowed to go abroad for medical treatment. Although this was an obvious ploy by Gorbachev to sweeten the atmosphere for the forthcoming Geneva summit in November, it was nevertheless exciting news and a definite victory for the Sakharov campaign.

It was later revealed that Mrs Bonner had agreed, as a condition of obtaining her visa, not to hold press conferences and to refrain from making anti-Soviet statements to the media while abroad. Sakharov himself signed a document stating that he accepted that the refusal of the Soviet authorities to allow him to travel abroad due to his possession of military secrets was reasonable. He also agreed to refrain in future from indulging in political activities unless in exceptional circumstances. What value statements of this kind really have when they are extracted under duress is open to question.

Another encouraging development was that Irina Grivnina, one of the original members of the Working Commission on the Abuse of Psychiatry whom we had been trying to defend for years, had been allowed to emigrate to Holland. She had been sentenced to five years' exile in 1981, but was allowed a remission after two years when she delivered herself of a baby. (One of the rare signs of humanity on the part of the Soviet system is that they rarely keep mothers of new-born babies in prison.) She arrived in Amsterdam on 29 October with her husband and two children. Again her release was a calculated move. It was obviously ordered in an attempt to influence the Dutch parliament against the acceptance of cruise missiles. In Amsterdam Grivnina received a heroine's welcome, which she richly deserved. A number of Dutch parliamentarians were among the welcomers. She was immediately offered an appointment as a special correspondent to a Dutch magazine.

A few weeks after arrival in the West Grivnina again hit the headlines when, on 18 November, she interrupted a Soviet press conference on arms control in Geneva. The Russian spokesman was being questioned about arms control verification procedures, but Grivnina insisted that she wanted to talk about human rights and the plight of the many people in the USSR 'condemned for anti-Soviet agitation'. It seems she got carried away and, although she succeeded in causing a stir, it was not really the most effective intervention she could have made. Finally, she did allow the arms control question to be answered but then rose again to ask about Anatoly Koryagin. When she repeated her interruptions next day, the Soviet delegation simply ended the press conference. All in all, it was perhaps a counter-productive effort. I later spoke about the episode to Robert van Voren, who had done more than any of us to obtain Grivnina's release, but all he would say was that she was 'very upset'.

Elena Bonner arrived in Milan on 3 December to be greeted by her son, Alexei, and son-in-law, Efrem. She declined to speak to reporters, saying that she feared that to breach the conditions of her visa would risk her being refused permission to return to her husband on the completion of her medical treatment – so much for the scandalous accusations made by *Izvestia* that she would walk over her husband's dead body to get to the West.

In February 1986, Elena Bonner underwent an operation for severe coronary sclerosis at the Massachusetts General Hospital. It was necessary to by-pass six blockages in her coronary arteries. The most important contribution which she made to her medical progress was to discontinue smoking – she had tried to do this in the USSR but the combination of emotional pressures upon her made it impossible. She made a rapid recovery from the surgery and within a few weeks was able to convalesce in the Virgin Islands where she went with Ed Kline and his wife. It was during this holiday in idyllic conditions that she wrote most of the book which she subsequently published with the title of *Alone Together*.

With the release of Mrs Bonner, I felt that a highly significant change had occurred in the Sakharov case. No longer would we be in the dark; we would know, and the world would know, what had happened to Sakharov. Things could no longer be the same. His release from exile could only be a matter of time – the time needed for face saving – because it no longer served any purpose and was a constant focus for scandalized reproach by the world's leaders and public opinion in general.

The developments of the next ten months were recorded in the extracts from my diary which follow.

7 February

I attended a special luncheon at the Institute of Physics to commemorate the ninth anniversary of the imprisonment and exile of Yuri Orlov. I felt an intense wave of depression at the memory of the optimistic meeting I had had in Moscow with his devoted wife Irina in 1977, when I predicted that the enormous concern in the scientific community and elsewhere for Orlov would ensure his early release from prison. How wrong this prediction has proved to be.*

One thing which cheered me up was that Valentin Turchin was to be at the lunch. I looked forward to meeting this charming man who would doubtless be able to give me the latest information about the Sakharovs. [We dined together after the meeting and he did indeed give me much important news on the human rights situation in the USSR with which he remained closely in touch.] The luncheon had been arranged by John Macdonald QC who has fought virtually single-handed to keep the Orlov affair before the public. The gathering was addressed by John Eades who reported that his fellow scientists at CERN, the cooperative European nuclear research centre, are threatening to withdraw from scientific contact with their Soviet colleagues if Orlov's prison sentence, due to end now, is prolonged further.

30 April

I arrived in New York with the purpose of visiting Elena Bonner in Boston. But my first appointment was with Ed Kline with whom I had lunch, and later a long slow walk back to my hotel across Central Park. Ed has been confidant and adviser to the Sakharov family, and their most stalwart defender, since the beginning of their travail. He was for many years publisher of the

---

* Orlov was released in October 1986.

Khronika Press which, under the editorship of Valery Chalidze, was an important vehicle for emigré writers and the publisher of the *Chronicle of Current Events*. Ed brought me up to date with the latest news of the Sakharov saga, including the welcome information that Elena Bonner had benefited greatly from her surgery and was quite free of the disabling *angina pectoris* which had crippled her before the operation. In a sense I was relieved to know that all the agitation on her behalf had been properly founded.*

3 May

I flew to Boston and spent the afternoon with the Yankelevich family. Mrs Bonner was in sparkling form. She is a much more charismatic figure than I expected. Obviously the holiday and the time with her children and grandchildren have been of great benefit. She seemed highly intelligent and direct – like many Soviet dissidents. A no-nonsense person, tough, uncompromising, blunt to the point of rudeness, outspoken, analytical, interesting, impatient of triviality.

She has a character honed by unparalleled disasters and she is truly a survivor. With her father shot (by Stalin) and her mother imprisoned, she had been brought up by a grandmother. She had learned not to show feeling. But this did not mean that she felt nothing. She gave me a detailed account of Sakharov's health status, including the information that he had suffered a myocardial infarction [heart attack] in the past and suffered from moderate high blood pressure. This was controlled by a small dose of rawalfia, a drug long since discarded in the West because of its tendency to produce depression. Apparently Sakharov did not react adversely to it and it kept his blood pressure within the normal range where more sophisticated drugs did not. We talked about future strategies for helping Sakharov, but not in any detail or with conviction.

Reagan's refusal to meet her in Washington (she was shunted

---

* Later the Soviets would claim that by-pass surgery was freely available to Soviet citizens and that Mrs Bonner had no need to go abroad for it. This was quite untrue – it may have been available to senior members of the *Nomenklatura*, but certainly not to the public. In any case, Mrs Bonner did not trust the doctors who had more than once demonstrated their subservience to the KGB.

off to see the National Security Adviser, Poindexter) had made her somewhat depressed. Apparently Reagan had acted on the advice of Richard Nixon who said a meeting with Bonner would send the wrong signal – the Russians had let her out to indicate that they were looking for a better relationship with the US; Reagan should show his appreciation by not getting directly involved with her. I offered to try and arrange a meeting with Mrs Thatcher who I knew would be under no such restrictions and this cheered everybody up.

Back at my hotel I rang Martin Dewhirst and asked him to contact the Prime Minister's office. This he did at once and I was able to confirm that Mrs Thatcher had agreed a meeting at Downing Street for Mrs Bonner on 30 May, a date which she could fit into her schedule before flying back to Gorky.

8 May

I flew down to Washington to attend, as a non-psychiatric observer, the Annual Meeting of the American Psychiatric Association (APA). This is an enormous jamboree with something like 12,000 participants. I had an amusing and informative dinner beforehand with Ellen Mercer and Peter Reddaway. There is to be a special symposium on the psychiatric abuse question tomorrow, and there are strong indications that a number of the members of the APA are far from happy with the way things have been managed, in particular with the campaign which culminated in the Soviet resignation from the World Psychiatric Association. They feel the accusations of abuse have been carried too far – being psychiatrists, they feel uneasy about attributing guilt and blame; they are accustomed to analysing, but not to chastising, the wrongdoer. There is in fact a strong move to make conciliatory gestures towards the Soviets, preferably by individual psychiatrists rather than by the APA itself. Dr Boris Zoubok (a former Soviet psychiatrist) spoke out strongly in support of the existing policy as did Reddaway and Bloch. They were well supported and the move towards rehabilitation of the USSR has petered out (at least for the time being).

13 May

At their request I attended a meeting of the APA Committee on Psychiatric Abuse and listened to a detailed account by a Californian psychiatrist, Dr Ponomareff, who claims that he visited the Bekhterev institute in Leningrad (one of the most prestigious medical Institutes in the USSR) and that the staff there had no knowledge of the Koryagin affair. I found this quite unbelievable. The Bekhterev Institute is in a constant state of rivalry with the Moscow Psychiatric Institute and any scandal affecting the latter would be bound to create interest, and indeed some satisfaction, in the former. I pointed this out. There was general agreement with my view and a feeling that no approaches of any kind were justified towards the Soviet psychiatric profession while Koryagin remained under restraint.

14 May

I attended a special Senatorial enquiry at Raeburn House where Anatoly Shcharansky gave evidence on the human rights situation in the USSR. There can be no doubt that Shcharansky is a very special human being. He epitomizes the modern anti-hero – a small, dumpy figure, he is the absolute opposite of the Clint Eastwood image or for that matter the John Wayne style we have grown so accustomed to when we think of individuals who have the guts to defy 'the baddies'. Shcharansky's weapons, which the KGB found impossible to defeat, were his indomitable spirit, his fearlessness, his convictions, his religious faith and his humour. The story he tells of the physical mistreatment to which he (and many others) had been subjected was quite scandalous. There seems to me no doubt that, one day, another Nuremberg trial will be necessary to punish those who have inflicted such savage punishments on their fellow men. But of course, such a trial will be held by the Russians themselves when they finally come to grips with tyranny and decide they will not tolerate any more of it.

18 May

The *Sunday Times* has published an interview with Mrs Bonner, mainly about her feelings on being back in the US with her family. She starts off by saying that she is convinced the American people (like the Russian people) do not want war. How can they, when their most fervent desire is to own their own homes and to tend their gardens? This desire permeates every layer and class in

American society and reflects a passionate desire for privacy and
the right of individuals to be themselves, do their own thing and,
in short, to be independent. (It is clear that she is over-reacting to
the generations of over-crowding and control of housing which
have deprived the Soviet population of this most precious of
privileges, to say nothing of the complete loss of personal independence which is the *sine qua non* of Soviet citizenship.)

She then waxes rather lyrical about the beach and the coconut
palms of the Virgin Islands retreat which is the setting for her
interview. It cannot be difficult to feel that way after the rigours
of Gorky. But the whole scenario has taken on a surreal quality –
the lapping of the calm waters of the Atlantic, the soft silky sand
of the beach. She dreams of being free to own a house of her own,
something she has never had – not a big place, nothing grand, just
a few rooms for herself, her husband and space for her children
and grandchildren to visit her. Although a bit mawkish, this
account of her dreams is a very effective way of describing the
difference between being an American, to whom such dreams are
realizable, and a Soviet citizen, to whom they are not. Yet they
are truly universal human aspirations. Bonner makes one very
important statement in this interview, I thought: she says that
Sakharov told her, just before she left for America, 'the world is
further away from war than it has ever been.' I hope he is right. I
suspect he is.

21 May

The Parliamentary Human Rights Group, which comprises about
a hundred members of both the House of Commons and the
House of Lords, has obtained 65 signatures to a resolution calling
on Gorbachev to free Sakharov. It was issued today to coincide
with Sakharov's 65th birthday. The appeal continues with a
statement:

According to the information available to us, Dr Sakharov
has never been charged with an offence [which is true] and
his banishment to Gorky six years ago took place without a
trial or sentence. We understand that Sakharov has not been
privy to military secrets for seventeen years and on the basis
of the evidence of Western scientists, we do not believe he

would have residual knowledge of these matters which could harm the interests of the Soviet Union.

I was very pleased with this effort as the group has been rather inactive (or so it would seem) for some time past.

I received the text of a speech which Mrs Bonner gave at the Congress of the United States to commemorate this her husband's birthday; it contains some moving and important passages. She refers to their total isolation in Gorky and the mass of disinformation, including letters, telegrams and secretly made and fabricated films about them, which the KGB have sent out with the intention of showing the world that they are well and leading normal lives. She pleads that this be disregarded. Their lives are fraught with danger every day and anything can happen to them without the world knowing.

Speaking not as a wife, but as a contemporary of Andrei Sakharov, she explained that his struggle grew out of their times which had been characterized not only by devastating wars but by such horrendous events as the Holocaust, the Gulags, Katyn, Auschwitz and Hiroshima. Since these monstrous events, people have been trying to create conditions which will prevent their repetition. Sakharov has been in the forefront of that process. It is circumstances which have shaped him and made him the defender of mankind which he now is. She says, 'His basic premise is the indivisibility of peace, progress and human rights. His basic ideology is that the defence of human rights is necessary to the defence of life on earth.'

28 May

Mrs Bonner and Tanya Yankelevich arrived in London. Mrs Bonner remained tight-lipped, refusing to speak to the press. I could not see the point of this as she had spoken fairly freely in the US, including the address she gave to the Congress.

28 May

In an interview with President Mitterrand [27 May], Mrs Bonner repeated that Sakharov had given a written undertaking not to engage in political activities if he was allowed to return to Moscow and given an opportunity to resume his work. President Mitterrand gave her an assurance that he had taken careful note of this promise and would raise the Sakharov case at every possible opportunity with the Soviet authorities which, of course, he had done previously, and with considerable effect.

29 May

We gave a small party to enable Mrs Bonner to meet some of the people who had been so helpful in our campaign. These included Professor John Goodwin (the cardiologist who had offered his services to her), Charles Janson, the Countess of Sutherland, Lord Avebury (leader of the Human Rights Group in Parliament), Iain Elliot from *The Times* and other media figures. Tanya Litvinov and her daughters, Vera and Masha, were also there which made Mrs Bonner very happy.

About 5 p.m. I got a call from the BBC to say that the German newspaper *Bild*, which the KGB had previously used as a source for their disinformation films on the Sakharovs, had just shown a new film of Andrei Sakharov in Gorky. Apparently he is seen speaking to a reporter and to some passers-by in the street, and says, amongst other things, that Gorbachev's latest disarmament proposals are 'promising' and that SDI was unworkable because it could never be tested. He evidently says a great deal more and the BBC were anxious to hear Mrs Bonner's comments. I promised to discuss the matter with her when she arrived. Soon after, the producer of the Independent Television News also called with a similar request. I told him that I was sure that Mrs Bonner would say little, if anything, and certainly not unless a copy of the film was available. I thought this would end the matter but an hour later, Michael Brunson (the ITN foreign affairs specialist) rang to say a copy of the film was on its way by special courier.

When Mrs Bonner arrived, I spoke to her about the two requests that she should comment on the film. She refused point-blank, saying that she would have nothing whatsoever to do with what was clearly, like previous films, a KGB artefact. These secretly-made films were a very sore point with Mrs Bonner, who described them, quite rightly, as an intolerable invasion of privacy and a form of psychological torture which should be condemned. She said they made her feel like a microbe under a microscope. She was particularly incensed by one sequence which showed

Sakharov without his trousers, undressing for a medical examination. She described this as a gross breach of medical confidentiality and one which should earn the Soviets the condemnation of the world medical profession (which it did not).

When the film arrived Mrs Bonner refused, as I had predicted, even to view it. She asked me to do so and to make any comment I thought appropriate. The film was in many respects remarkably crude – for example, the concealed microphone was clearly visible to the viewer, if not to Sakharov, since it stuck out of a furled newspaper which projected from the reporter's groin like an erect penis. But what Sakharov said was interesting, to say the least. He spoke about Chernobyl – a disaster, but not one which should halt the nuclear programme, just as the Challenger explosion should not halt manned space exploration. It seemed as if he was anxious to equate every Soviet misfortune at the technical level with an equivalent failure in the West. He mentioned the nuclear accidents at Three Mile Island and at Windscale, saying they were like Chernobyl only smaller in effect. But certainly his most interesting comments were those concerned with nuclear disarmament – Gorbachev was on the right track and SDI was quite unrealistic.

The film is clearly a *montage* of different interviews filmed secretly and put together to show Sakharov as supporting the Gorbachev line. What Sakharov really thinks it would be impossible to say.

I told Michael Brunson in an interview that Mrs Bonner regarded the film as a KGB ploy and that she did not play games with the KGB. I added that if these were Sakharov's views, he should be put on a plane at once to Geneva to join the Soviet negotiating team.*

30 May

The meeting with Mrs Thatcher at 10 Downing Street was extraordinarily successful. I had expected it to be a pure formality, over in a few minutes after a ritual greeting and a press 'opportunity'. Quite the contrary. We were taken into Mrs Thatcher's

---

* It is possible that Sakharov's views on SDI played a part in the final decision to allow him to go free.

sitting room, given coffee and the Prime Minister listened carefully to Mrs Bonner for half an hour. She showed herself to be very well-informed and most concerned and she promised to raise the Sakharov matter at every opportunity (which she has in fact already done). After the interview Mrs Thatcher took us on a guided tour of Downing Street and into the Cabinet room, showing where she sat and chaired the proceedings. She then escorted Mrs Bonner across Downing Street to the crowd of reporters and TV cameramen waiting for interviews, and, holding her protectively by the arm, she told them that she felt that Mrs Bonner represented everything fine in the human spirit. She had defied enormous pressures in order to stand by her husband; she was one of humanity's great defenders.

Martin and I escorted Mrs Bonner and Tanya to the airport. The final leave-taking was heart-rending. They never expected to see each other again. Mrs Bonner displayed little emotion, just a stoic resignation to her fate. Tanya wept.

30 May

Victor Louis, a journalist who is widely regarded as simply a KGB mouthpiece, has said in a statement, made in Moscow and quoted in the *International Herald Tribune*, that there is clearly no further reason for keeping Sakharov in exile in Gorky, but his wife's public criticisms and other statements are jeopardizing the possibilities of the authorities making concessions to either of them. [This was a reference to Mrs Bonner's sight-seeing in London.] When later asked to comment on this statement Mrs Bonner was dismissive – referring to it as typical KGB blackmail. I described Louis' statement in *The Times* as:

A most brutal and damaging report designed to intimidate a sick woman who is desperate to help her husband. During her stay in the West Mrs Bonner had held no press conferences [so honouring her promise] and had made no statements damaging to the Soviet Union. She had confined her remarks to factual statements relating to their situation and its implications.

Another press report refers to the release from prison of

Alexander Shatravka and Dr Vladimir Brodsky, two important members of the independent nuclear disarmament body, the Moscow Trust Group. Dr Chazov has been quick to claim the credit for their release.

FINAL VICTORY?

Between June and December 1986 there was little activity in the Sakharov Campaign in the UK. I kept in touch with Ed Kline who told me that nothing had changed significantly in Gorky – the supervision was still strict, but more frequent, though closely monitored, telephone calls were permitted to the family in Newton. But I suspected that it was only a matter of time before the Sakharov exile would be ended. It didn't make sense any longer and only served as an irritant between Gorbachev and every Western leader who came into contact with him. But Gorbachev still had to contend with his hard-liners.

When success came it was swift and unexpected. On 19 December 1986 Andrei Sakharov and Mrs Bonner were given permission to return to Moscow. The news was conveyed to them personally by Mikhail Gorbachev after a telephone had been installed in their apartment in Gorky. Sakharov apparently told Gorbachev that, despite the reprieve, he had no intention of abandoning his commitment to the human rights struggle. He wished to resume his scientific work at the Institute of Physics but would not remain silent in the face of abuses of which he disapproved. He called for the immediate release of political prisoners in the USSR and the ending of the Soviet intervention in Afghanistan. So nothing has changed. Sakharov was older and physically weaker, but still as staunch in his defence of humanity as ever. That was the victory. The demonstration that the human spirit cannot be conquered even by the most ruthless power. Thus hope survives.

London, 21 December 1986.

INDEX